THE ANXIETY FIX

LEE ANN THOMSON

 FriesenPress

Suite 300 - 990 Fort St
Victoria, BC, V8V 3K2
Canada

www.friesenpress.com

ISBN
978-1-5255-8797-9 (Hardcover)
978-1-5255-8796-2 (Paperback)
978-1-5255-8798-6 (eBook)

1. SELF-HELP, ANXIETIES & PHOBIAS

Distributed to the trade by The Ingram Book Company

The Anxiety Fix consists of this book and an audio recording for you to download.

The audio recording is not only essential to your success, it is also enjoyable and relaxing. Listen to it daily to reinforce your neural pathways, eliminate anxiety, and solidify your success.

To access and download the audio recording portion of this program:
1. Go to https://okhypno.ca/book-audio/
2. Input the following password: 1MAgNGd!9qte

Do not listen to this recording while driving or operating machinery.

Enjoy the techniques and relax knowing that you are on your way to lasting success eliminating your anxiety.

Important: This book is not intended as a substitute for medical or psychological advice or treatment. Any person with a condition requiring medical or psychological treatment should consult a medical practitioner or suitable therapist. Do not stop taking any medications without medical supervision.

DEDICATION

To my husband, Mike, the love of my life,
who encourages me every step along the journey with love,
humour, and wisdom – thank you.
I also like to thank Maciej (Magic) Komuniecki
for his friendship and good natured IT support.

CONTENTS

INTRODUCTION   1

CHAPTER 1   5
Understanding anxiety   5
Anxiety can be normal and beneficial   6
Anxiety can become a problem   6
What is the difference between fear and anxiety?   7
What are the symptoms?   8
The anxious brain   9
The evolution of anxiety: Why we worry   10
How anxiety works   11
How avoidance leads to fear learning and more anxiety   12
How to use safety learning to decrease anxiety   14
Avoidance   15

CHAPTER 2   17
Anxiety comes in many forms   17
Generalized anxiety   17
Social anxiety   20
Agoraphobia   20
Panic attacks   21
Separation anxiety   22
Specific phobias   22
Obsessive-Compulsive Disorder (OCD)   23
Post-Traumatic Stress Disorder (PTSD)   24
Hangover anxiety   25
Marijuana-related anxiety   25

CHAPTER 3   27
  What causes anxiety?   27
  Stress   28
  Trauma   28
  Serious health events and chronic illness   28
  Alcohol and drug use   29
  Medical conditions related to ageing   29
  Is it anxiety or is it something else?   29
  Blood sugar imbalance   29
  Nutrient deficiencies and anxiety   31
  Microbiome imbalance   32
  Is your past controlling your anxiety?   33
  Repeat   34
  React   35
  Re-create   35
  Does anxiety come from nature or nurture?   37

CHAPTER 4   39
  We are all affected by anxiety   39
  Employees   40
  College students   40
  Gay, bisexual, and transgender people   40
  Aboriginal people   41
  Young adults   41
  New parents   41
  Older men and women   42
  Unemployed people   42
  Health and chronic illness   42
  What age group is most affected by anxiety?   43
  Is there such a thing as an anxious personality?   43
  Gender and Anxiety   44
  Sex and Anxiety   45

CHAPTER 5   47
  Your brain, memory, and neuroplasticity   47
  Hebb's Law   48

Your brain's tendency to generalize   48
Quantum zeno effect   51
We want to know why we are anxious   52
We can't change the past   52

CHAPTER 6   55

Memory: Can you trust yours?   55
Attention or mindfulness   56
Learning and the reward circuit   57
Learning and sleep   58
Memory consolidation and synapses   59
Influences on the memory consolidation process   60
Memory distribution   60
Episodic memory   61
Memory reconsolidation   62
Your memory changes every time you access it   63
Memory distortion   66
Schemas   66
Source amnesia   67
The misinformation effect   67
Hindsight bias   68
The overconfidence effect   68
Confabulation   68

CHAPTER 7   71

Is your brain playing tricks on you?   71
Optical illusions   71
Is your mind playing tricks on you?   73
Cognitive Distortions   73
Reframing 13 common cognitive distortions   74

CHAPTER 8   81

Neuroplasticity – your brain's superpower   81
Self-directed neuroplasticity   83
Experience-dependent neuroplasticity   83
Neural pathways   84

CHAPTER 9   87
   Effective therapies for anxiety   87
   Cognitive Behaviour Therapy   87
   Hypnotherapy   89
   Hypnosis and neural pathways   90
   Combining Cognitive Behaviour Therapy and Hypnosis   91
   Mindfulness   92
   Combining Cognitive Behaviour Therapy and Mindfulness   94
   Cognitive Behaviour Therapy, Mindfulness, and Hypnosis
   as a treatment method for anxiety   94
   Making the sum greater than the whole   96

CHAPTER 10   97
   The Anxiety Fix Toolkit   97
   Pattern-interrupt techniques   98
   Mindfulness   98
   Bilateral stimulation   100
   Deep and slow breathing (and your vagus nerve)   101
   Peripheral vision   102
   Changing internal dialogue   102
   Reframing   103

CHAPTER 11   105
   How long does it take to form a new habit and
   change a neural pathway?   105
   Finding inspiration   107
   Where to go from here   108
   Maintenance   109

SOURCES   111

INTRODUCTION

You have been dreaming of a life without anxiety. You may remember and long for a time in your life before anxiety got its tenacious grip on you. You may have tried a number of ways to cope with your anxiety: medication, aromatherapy, yoga, journaling, supplements, diet, or just denying it. You have tried it all. Yet despite your efforts, you are still suffering its crippling effects.

While anxiety has many forms and many causes, every type of anxiety has one thing in common: the neural pathways within your brain. Neural pathways are similar to hiking trails. Just as a grassy path becomes flattened, matted, and wider every time a hiker walks over it, your neural pathways are created and strengthened by your thoughts, feelings, and beliefs.

For example, when you experience a real or imagined threat (like a barking dog), your mind immediately goes down the neural pathway (think highway) to the anxiety response (fear/panic). The more times you experience this threat (barking dog), the more times you go into the fight or flight mode. Pretty soon, the pathway is large and wide, and every time you see a dog – whether it is barking or not – you automatically go into an anxious state.

The good news is that you can change your neural pathways!

How is it possible to change your neural pathways? Through neural plasticity. Neural plasticity is the brain's ability to change and adapt as a result of experiences. The information and Toolkit in this book and the accompanying audio recording will help you re-route your neural pathways and create new ones. So when you experience something that used to cause anxiety, your new neural pathways will travel down a path toward calmness.

Research has shown that combining three of the most powerful methods of treating anxiety, Cognitive Behaviour Therapy, Hypnosis, and Mindfulness – is an effective, long-lasting treatment. *The Anxiety Fix* explains these three treatments and integrates them into an approach referred to as Mindfulness based Cognitive Behaviour Hypnotherapy.

As a Registered Clinical Counselling Hypnotherapist, I have used these therapies to eliminate anxiety in many clients. One of my favourite clients, Emily, was afraid to drive and frightened of dogs (even her own dogs). She was afraid to leave her house. Her world was slowly closing in. By using therapies explained in *The Anxiety Fix*, she has her life back. Now, Emily not only drives, her confidence is so high that she recently successfully ran for political office. Not long ago, she sent me a picture of herself smiling with her dogs in her car as they were heading out for a drive.

I wrote this book to help the countless people who don't seek treatment for their anxiety because of stigma, shame, or logistical barriers. There is nothing standing in your way of taking back your life. *The Anxiety Fix* provides you with the information and tools you need to understand how anxiety and your brain work, change the way you think, alter your neural pathways, and take control of your anxiety.

You can eliminate your anxiety from the privacy of your own home by relaxing, listening to the audio recording, and using the Toolkit techniques in this book to make permanent, positive changes to your thought patterns and neural pathways.

Take your life back!

Lee Ann Thomson
Registered Clinical Counselling Hypnotherapist

In computer terms, anxiety is both a hardware problem
(I'm wired badly) and a software problem
(I run faulty logic programs that make me think
anxious thoughts).

—Scott Stossell, *My Age of Anxiety*

CHAPTER 1

Understanding anxiety

Anxiety can be crippling and as confusing to understand as it is distressing to experience. We are all affected by anxiety, whether it is our own or someone else's. We are all touched by it on a regular basis, yet we don't talk to our friends, families, or doctors about it, and we don't teach our children about it so they are better able to deal with it.

Why is a naturally occurring problem that affects so many people so misunderstood and taboo to discuss? Stigma, shame, and logistical barriers stop many from seeking help. Countless people with anxiety don't ever seek treatment. In an effort to identify what stands in their way of getting help with anxiety, researchers surveyed 226 adults with untreated anxiety disorders about their reasons for not seeking treatment. The four leading reasons given by those with generalized anxiety disorders are:

81% wanted to handle problems on their own
75% felt embarrassed about needing help
74% didn't know where to go for treatment
74% thought the cost would be too high

Anxiety can be normal and beneficial

Everyone deals with anxiety at one time or another. It activates our fight or flight response. It warns us when we might be in danger and can help us get away from it. There are an infinite number of human experiences that cause anxiety. Life offers us the experience of many anxiety-provoking "firsts", such as a first date, the first day of school, and the first time away from home.

As we journey through life, there are many important life events, both good and bad, that cause varying amounts of anxiety. These events can include things such as taking an exam, getting married, becoming a parent, getting divorced, changing jobs, coping with illness, and many others.

The discomfort anxiety brings in these situations is considered normal and even beneficial. Anxiety about an upcoming test may cause you to work harder to prepare for the exam. The anxiety you feel when walking through a dark and deserted parking lot to your car will cause you to be alert and cautious of your surroundings, or better yet, to get an escort to your vehicle.

Anxiety can become a problem

While it is clear to see that anxiety is normal and even beneficial, for many people it becomes a problem. The main difference between normal anxiety and problem anxiety is the intensity of the experience. Anxiety can prevent us from living life to its fullest.

Normal anxiety is intermittent and is expected based on certain events or situations. Problem anxiety, on the other hand, tends to be chronic and irrational and interferes with many life functions. Avoidance behaviour, incessant worry, as well as concentration and memory problems may all stem from problem anxiety. These symptoms may be so intense that they cause family, work, and social difficulties.

The components of problem anxiety include physical responses to the anxiety (such as palpitations and stomach upset), distorted thoughts that become a source of excessive worry, and behavioural changes that affect the usual way one lives life and interacts with others. Left unchecked, problem anxiety may lead to an anxiety disorder.

What is the difference between fear and anxiety?

Anxiety is a normal emotion that is essential for survival. However, for some individuals, it is as if their anxiety has a life of its own, getting triggered by the least provocation, like an overly sensitive car alarm that gets activated each time a leaf falls on the hood.

Simply put: *Fear* relates to a known or understood threat, whereas *anxiety* follows from an unknown or poorly defined threat.

Fear is an emotional response to a known or definite threat. For example, if you are walking down a dark street and someone points a gun at you and says, "Give me your wallet," you would likely experience a fear response. The danger is real, definite, and immediate. There is a clear and present object of the fear.

Anxiety is an unpleasant, vague sense of apprehension. It is often a response to an imprecise or unknown threat. For example, imagine you are walking down a dark street. You may feel a little uneasy and have a few butterflies in your stomach. These sensations are caused by anxiety that is related to the *possibility* that a stranger might jump out and harm you. This anxiety is not the result of a known or specific threat. Rather it comes from your mind's interpretation of the possible dangers that could immediately occur.

Although the focus of the response is different (real vs. imagined danger), fear and anxiety are interrelated. Fear causes anxiety, and anxiety can cause fear. But the subtle distinctions between the two can give you a better understanding of your responses. When faced with anxiety most people will experience the physical reactions that are associated with fear.

Everyone feels anxiety at times. When we think something bad is about to happen, we react as if something bad is happening, even when it is not true. We also start focusing on the bad side of things. These negative thoughts add up. Soon, a small problem feels like a very big problem. This can make anxiety even worse.

What are the symptoms?

Millions of people around the world experience anxiety every day. You may be familiar with or have experienced some of these symptoms of anxiety:

- feelings of being out of control of your health and life
- higher levels of overall stress
- struggles with low self-esteem
- nervousness in social situations
- difficulty managing pressure
- high expectations of yourself and others
- unhealthy boundaries
- workaholic tendencies
- frequent illnesses and doctor visits
- unhealthy relationships
- overall unhappiness
- erratic emotional behaviours
- being quick to anger
- regular feelings of being unsettled
- regular feelings of being overwhelmed
- a sense of being disconnected and detached from life or that life is passing you by
- a tendency to be unreliable (because your symptoms may prevent you from following through)

Anxious people also often:

- jump from relationship to relationship in search of perfection
- jump from job to job because of higher levels of stress
- live a restricted lifestyle (within a self-imposed "safe zone")

Ongoing anxiety can cause considerable worry or interference in everyday life. It can prevent you from engaging in routine daily activities or meeting expected personal milestones. You may be too afraid to pursue a promotion or apply for a new job or pretend to be busy on the weekends because dating and socializing seem terrifying.

So, where does anxiety start?

The anxious brain

The source of anxiety is the brain, the anxious brain. Although we are still a long way from fully understanding what is going on in an anxious brain, recent studies offer some insights into why anxiety seems to take over in some people. Central to it all is the amygdala, the brain region that processes our emotions and triggers the release of the hormones responsible for the fight-or-flight response.

The amygdala is linked to parts of the prefrontal and anterior cingulate cortex that process social information and help us to make decisions. During bouts of everyday anxiety, this brain circuit switches on and then off again – but Oliver Robinson and his colleagues at University College London have shown that in people with anxiety disorders this brain circuit seems to get stuck in the on position. "We think it might be amplifying negative information in your surround-ings to make sure you pay attention to it and triggering a fight-or-flight response, so you'll run away," says Robinson.

Studies suggest that fear memories stored in the amygdala prime us to respond to threats we have previously experienced. This response is normally kept in check by a parallel circuit. In healthy people, inputs from the prefrontal cortex can temper our learned response and even overwrite it with new memories. Occasionally the system fails, however. Psychiatrists have found that war veterans with Post-Traumatic Stress Disorder – a kind of anxiety disorder – have abnormally low levels of activity in their prefrontal cortex and unusually high levels in their amygdala.

Ultimately, an overactive amygdala appears to hype up the familiar symptoms of the fight-or-flight response by stimulating a network of hormonal glands and brain regions, causing rapid heart rate and breathing, a dry mouth, shaking, and tense muscles. The fight-or-flight response also has less obvious effects, like slowing digestion and making us more susceptible to pain. Let's look at how anxiety evolved in the human race.

The evolution of anxiety: Why we worry

The earliest remains of modern humans are approximately 200,000 years old. These were the first Homo sapiens to have a brain relatively similar to ours. In particular, the neocortex – the newest part of the brain and the region responsible for higher functions like language – was roughly the same size 200,000 years ago as it is today. You are walking around with the same hardware as your Paleolithic ancestors.

Thousands of years ago, when humans lived in what scientists call an "immediate return environment", stress and anxiety were useful emotions because they helped us take action in the face of immediate problems. On any given day, your ancestors were constantly focused on things like what to eat, where to sleep, and how to avoid a predator – things that made an immediate impact on their lives. In this immediate return environment, their choices delivered clear and immediate outcomes.

For example:
- A lion appears across the plain > you feel stressed > you run away > your stress is relieved.
- A storm rumbles in the distance > you worry about finding shelter > you find shelter > your anxiety is relieved.
- You haven't drunk any water today > you feel stressed and dehydrated > you find water > your stress is relieved.

This is how your brain evolved to use worry, anxiety, and stress. Anxiety was an emotion that helped protect humans in an immediate return environment and solve short-term, acute problems. There was no such thing as chronic stress because there aren't chronic problems in an immediate return environment.

Wild animals rarely experience chronic stress. As Duke University professor Mark Leary put it, "A deer may be startled by a loud noise and take off through the forest, but as soon as the threat is gone, the deer immediately calms down and starts grazing. It doesn't appear to be tied in knots the way that many people are." When you live in an immediate return environment, you only have to worry about acute stressors. Once the threat is gone, the anxiety subsides.

Compared to the age of the brain, modern society is relatively new. It is only during the last 500 years or so that our society has shifted to a predominantly "delayed return environment". While lots can happen in 500 years, from the perspective of evolution, 500 years is nothing. The modern human brain spent hundreds of thousands of years evolving for one type of environment (immediate returns), and in the blink of an eye, the entire environment changed (delayed returns). Your brain is wired to value immediate returns.

Our brains didn't evolve in a delayed return environment, but that is where we find ourselves today. Today we face different problems. Many of the choices you make today will not benefit you immediately. Will you have enough money to pay the bills next month? Will you get the promotion at work or remain stuck in your current job? Can you repair a broken relationship? Problems in a delayed return environment can rarely be solved *right now* in the present. In fact, many aspects of modern society are designed to delay rewards until some point in the future. For example, if you do a good job at work today, you will get paid in a few weeks, or if you save money now, you will have enough for retirement later.

Unfortunately, living in a delayed return environment tends to lead to chronic stress and anxiety for humans because our brains did not evolve to solve the problems of a delayed return environment.

How anxiety works

The single most important issue when it comes to anxiety is avoidance. More specifically, the reason clinical levels of anxiety persist is because we try to avoid our anxiety in the first place.

At their core, all anxiety disorders are basically the same. Even though they may look and – to some extent – feel very different, from a mechanical perspective, the same dynamics are present. That is, people with anxiety disorders have trained themselves to be afraid of the thoughts, sensations, and emotions associated with anxiety, and they have done this quite by accident. In fact, the very thing they do to try and make their anxiety better – avoiding it – is the thing that is counter intuitively making it worse.

To explain how all this works, we need to take a better look at how the part of the brain called the amygdala works. The amygdala's main job is to keep us safe from danger – specifically, physical threats to our survival. To do this, it is always on the lookout for potential threats and constantly scanning the environment for suspicious activity. If it spots something that it thinks might be dangerous, it sounds the alarm and prepares our bodies to deal with the potential threat. It does this by stimulating the autonomic nervous system to release adrenaline and activate our fight-or-flight response. Our breathing gets faster, our heart rate goes up, muscles tense, and blood flows quickly out of the torso and head and into our extremities so that we can more efficiently deliver oxygen to our arms and legs to either fight or flee.

Now, this is great if you are being confronted with a genuine physical threat to your survival –such as someone pulling a knife on you in a dark alley or a grizzly bear jumping out at you. In that case, you'd better hope your little amygdala gives you a lot of adrenaline to get out of there or to fight back. Obviously, adrenaline and our fight-or-flight response can be extremely helpful when confronted with a true threat to our survival.

The problems start when our amygdala gets confused about what types of things are truly threats to our survival – and therefore worthy of a full-blown fight-or-flight response – and things that maybe look or feel like threats but aren't actually dangerous or capable of hurting us.

How avoidance leads to fear learning and more anxiety

Most of us would agree that hiking is not typically a very dangerous activity. And while there is always the risk of falling off a cliff or getting attacked by a dangerous wild animal, in most scenarios going for a hike is a safe activity.

Yet, many people are too anxious to go hiking. They turn down invitations to hike or only go for walks in well-known paths or areas;

they even avoid movies about hiking and travelling through nature. *They believe that it makes sense to be afraid of something as good for you as hiking because that is what their amygdala believes.* And to a large extent, your amygdala tends to believe what you teach it.

People with anxiety disorders have most likely triggered a process called "fear learning", which has taught their amygdala to be overly sensitive to potential dangers and fear things that are not actually threatening. Imagine that you are out for a hike on a beautiful spring day. After being out for 20 or 30 minutes, you notice something up ahead of you – a dark, curvy line on the trail. Chances are your amygdala fires up a bit, warning you of a potential threat. (It could be a poisonous snake!) You feel your heart beat a little faster, and your muscles tense a bit. Maybe your chest feels a little tight. What you end up doing next is crucial when it comes to anxiety.

In addition to scanning the environment for potential threats and releasing adrenaline in order to prepare you to fight or flee if necessary, your amygdala has an error correction mechanism built in that allows it to learn when it has correctly or incorrectly flagged something as dangerous. This mechanism involves watching how you respond to the potential threat and using your behaviour to either confirm or deny its initial threat assessment. Specifically, it watches to see whether you try to avoid or approach the potentially dangerous thing.

If you avoid the thing the amygdala singled out as a danger – by either fighting it or running away from it – you are engaging in fear learning. In effect, you are telling your amygdala, "Yes, that thing you thought was dangerous is a genuine threat to my safety and survival. Remember it for next time and shoot me up with lots of adrenaline so I can run away faster."

If you attempt to avoid the potential threat – in this case running back down the trail away from the dark line – your anxiety will initially go down because the perceived threat is eliminated. But your amygdala interprets this action as confirmation that its initial assessment of the potential threat was accurate and that it was an actual threat; dark curvy lines on hiking trails are really dangerous! Consequently, your long-term levels of anxiety around hiking start to increase. The next time you go hiking, your amygdala will be even more on the lookout for dangerous snakes in the form of dark curvy lines and trigger a fight-or-flight response much faster.

Pretty soon, you are likely to start going on less adventurous hikes and possibly even avoid hiking all together because the mere thought of a hike triggers so much anxiety. Each time you constrict your range of activities, you are teaching your amygdala that hiking is an extremely dangerous activity. Before you know it, you have got a snake/hiking phobia or panic disorder.

To sum it up, fear learning occurs when your behaviour confirms your amygdala's initial assessment of a threat. Of course, sometimes fear learning is a good thing. If there truly is a danger present in a situation, you want your amygdala to remember it. But anxiety develops when the fear learning process is applied to things that may look or feel dangerous, but in reality are not.

Thankfully, the same mechanism the amygdala uses for fear learning can be applied to achieve the opposite, safety learning, which is the key to undoing any anxiety you may have developed.

How to use safety learning to decrease anxiety

If avoidance behaviour (e.g., running away) leads to fear learning, then approach behaviour is what leads to safety learning and a lessening of anxiety.

Let's go back to the hiking example. You initially see a dark curvy line ahead of you on the trail and feel a bit nervous. The thought crosses your mind that you could just turn back or maybe find a different path. But this time you just wait and watch. After 20 seconds, you notice that the line hasn't moved, so you take a few steps closer. You feel a bit more afraid, but you are curious and willing to check things out a little bit further.

You can now see that the line is moving a little, but in a strange way – not at all like a snake would. It looks like it is swaying. A few more steps and you now realize the dark shadowy line is actually a shadow from an overhanging tree limb. Not only does your fear immediately evaporate, but you have also taught your amygdala a valuable lesson: sometimes while hiking, what looks like a snake from a distance is often just a shadow. As a result, the next time you are out hiking, your amygdala will be a little more relaxed and your fight-or-flight response will be a little less likely to be triggered – all of which means you are more able to have fun and enjoy your hike. This is safety learning.

So, while avoiding things that look and feel like threats is often anxiety-relieving in the short term, it reinforces unrealistic beliefs in the long term that lead to both unnecessarily high and persistent anxiety as well as an increasingly restricted (and much less enjoyable) life. On the other hand, when we simply pause and observe, we get the chance to learn and obtain new information. If it turns out that the amygdala was right, then we can fight or flee appropriately. But if we learn that it was incorrect, it gets smarter, and we get less anxious.

Avoidance

Avoidance is the key factor in sustained and intense levels of anxiety because it mistakenly teaches the amygdala to respond to non-threats as though they were real threats. But behavioural avoidance – running away from a dark curvy line – is not the only way we avoid things. In fact, most of the time our anxiety is sustained or exacerbated by cognitive avoidance, and the most common form of this is worry.

But how can worry be "avoidance"? It almost seems like the opposite: Going over and over the scary thing in your mind is trying to solve the problem of what to do in a particular situation. But, unfortunately, worry is not problem solving. Worry gives us the illusion of control and the hope that we can make things better, but really it serves a different purpose – distraction. Worry keeps our mind off the feelings (emotional and physical) of anxiety. It lets us avoid them by thinking about the (perceived) problem. Unfortunately, by avoiding the feelings of anxiety (the symptoms of fight or flight) we are teaching our amygdala that the scary thing is dangerous and threatening to our survival.

This is the anxious person's dilemma. It is hard enough to be irrationally afraid of genuinely harmless situations, but to also be irrationally afraid of our own emotions and feelings makes daily life a constant struggle since our thoughts and feelings are always close at hand.

If it seems hard to tell whether something is avoidance (and therefore making your anxiety worse in the long run), just ask yourself this one question: *What am I teaching my amygdala?*

- What am I teaching my amygdala about plane flights when I pop a Xanax 5 minutes before I board my plane?
- What am I teaching my amygdala about crowds when I consistently decline invitations to hang out with friends in crowded environments?
- What am I teaching my amygdala about unfamiliar situations when I think through all the possible worst-case scenarios associated with starting a new job?
- What am I teaching my amygdala about sleep when I spend 30 minutes every night checking off items from my sleep hygiene list?
- What am I teaching my amygdala about my own anxiety when I habitually read articles online about anxiety whenever I start to feel nervous?

When you avoid something in response to anxiety, you are teaching your amygdala to fear and avoid harmless situations and creating strong neural pathways for the anxiety to travel down each time you encounter a trigger situation.

As you can see anxiety can be beneficial or harmful. Knowing the difference between fear and anxiety is an important factor in dealing with anxiety. It helps us to understand how safety learning is a positive response.

By understanding how your brain, mind, and neural pathways work, you can control and conquer your anxiety.

CHAPTER 2

Anxiety comes in many forms

Not everyone experiences anxiety in the same way. The type and intensity vary from person to person. You can experience more than one type of anxiety separately or simultaneously. The term "anxiety" is often used as a blanket term to cover all anxiety disorders. But the reality is that there are many different types of anxiety, and there are many different ways that you can experience anxiety-related symptoms.

Panic disorder is different from generalized anxiety disorder, which is different from social anxiety disorder, and so on. So even though these disorders are all referred to as "anxiety", they are different disorders, each with their own set of symptoms (although sometimes the symptoms overlap). This brings up an interesting question: Can you have more than one anxiety disorder? The answer is yes, and we will now look at some of the common forms of anxiety.

Generalized anxiety

People with generalized anxiety worry excessively about the outcome of events. Long before the time in question, they become preoccupied with the numerous possibilities and outcomes, regardless of the plausibility of these invented scenarios. They worry excessively about money, health, family, and/or work, even when there are no signs of trouble.

Generalized anxiety can be hard to diagnose. The symptoms are relatively unfocused; the nervousness is low-key and chronic; there are no panic attacks. It is, after all, "just worry", and that is something that touches all of us. But there are differences. Ordinary worry is less serious, and we are able (most of the time) to put it aside and concentrate on other, more immediate issues. However, generalized anxiety often starts, seemingly, without cause.

Although some people with generalized anxiety may be able to state what it is that makes them nervous, others can't. Generalized anxiety is typically about far more issues ("everything") than one particular subject. People with this disorder worry about vague what-ifs, have difficulty concentrating, and are unfocused. The disorder typically begins at about age 30, and many people with generalized anxiety have been asymptomatic for years, possibly because the degree of impairment is often not that severe.

People with general anxiety disorders are often indecisive. This indecisiveness is not limited to circumstances with numerous options to choose from - it extends to daily tasks as well. These people often exhibit nervousness when confronted with any choice and find it challenging to arrive at a satisfying decision. Even when they finally make a choice, they may still worry. Ordinary activities like choosing an outfit for a special occasion, buying a gift, or picking an item on the menu can be a lengthy process for people with general anxiety disorder. This symptom, though very common, is not often recognized as symptomatic of an anxiety disorder. It is often written off as the person being finicky or choosy.

In addition to both real and imagined situations, people with generalized anxiety also worry about worrying. They are usually aware of their anxious nature and thus stress about their mental state preemptively. For instance, when confronted with a future event, they worry about how stressed they are going to be. This vicious cycle can become incapacitating.

Enduring mental stress can affect physical health. Many people with generalized anxiety disorder experience fatigue, irritability, and headaches. Mental tension may also provoke muscle tension, leading to frequent aches and pains throughout the body. Stressful situations may cause a person to feel claustrophobic or nauseous. Other than these common physical manifestations, trembling, twitching, and easy startling are also possible.

Another common complaint from individuals with anxiety disorders is profuse sweating. Though sweating is normal to a certain extent, especially with physical activity or warm environments, profuse sweating without any exertion or activity is a sign that something is wrong.

General anxiety can cause palpitations, light-headedness, shortness of breath, and sometimes loss of consciousness. Struggling to breathe without physical exertion is a sign of an anxiety attack. In most cases, slow and deep breathing relieves the feeling of shortness of breath. Breathing slowly may feel counterintuitive, but it often works. However, anyone who experiences repeated instances of shortness of breath, palpitations, fainting, or light-headedness should see a health professional immediately.

Many people with general anxiety have intermittent insomnia. They struggle to fall asleep because their minds are racing. It is normal to wake up in the middle of the night with anticipatory anxiety right before a big presentation. However, frequently lying awake without any substantial reason could indicate general anxiety. Almost 50% of people with general anxiety report sleeping problems.

Though anxiety starts in the mind, it manifests with physical symptoms. In severe cases, people with general anxiety develop diarrhea and irritable bowel syndrome (IBS). IBS causes cramping, constipation, and bloating, as well as stomach aches.

Females are twice as likely to be afflicted than males. It is believed that the number of males who struggle with generalized anxiety is much higher because many don't report it to their doctors.

Social anxiety

People with social anxiety experience high levels of anxiety, fear, and avoidance of social situations due to feelings of embarrassment, self-consciousness, and concern about being judged or viewed negatively by others.

Social anxiety is a fear of appearing incompetent, unintelligent, or silly. People fear situations such as choking when eating in public, trembling when writing, or being unable to perform when speaking or playing a musical instrument in front of an audience. Because these activities almost always provoke disproportionate fear of embarrassment or social rejection, the person avoids these situations or endures them with much anxiety.

Using a public urinal can cause anxiety for some men. Fear of blushing especially affects women. Fear of choking is acquired after an episode of choking on food; it can occur anytime from childhood to old age.

Many people, both men and women, have noticeable physical symptoms with social anxiety: blushing, hoarseness, tremors, and sweating. Some people may have actual panic attacks. Studies of general populations report a lifetime occurrence of social anxiety ranging from 4% to as high as 13%. Onset is typically in the middle teens, can last for years, and has been reported to have a genetic basis. It is equally common among males and females.

Agoraphobia

A person with agoraphobia has a fear of any situation or place where escape seems awkward or embarrassing, or where help might be unavailable if anxiety symptoms should occur. These people almost invariably experience excessive anxiety or dread when they have to be alone or away from home. There is an abundance of potential opportunities for agoraphobia to occur: riding a bus (or other mass transit), shopping, or going to a movie. For some, it can occur when walking through an open space (flea market, playground), being part of a crowd, or standing in a line-up. So, they avoid such situations or confront them only with a trusted friend or, if all else fails, endure them with a lot of suffering.

As with panic attacks, women are more susceptible than men. Agoraphobia usually develops in the teens or twenties, though some people have their first symptoms after the age of 40. Often panic attacks precede the onset of agoraphobia. It is strongly heritable.

Panic attacks

A panic attack is fear, sometimes even stark terror, that comes on suddenly. It is accompanied by classic fight-or-flight symptoms. The person may experience feelings of impending doom, chest pain, chills, feeling too hot, choking, shortness of breath, and heart pounding or palpitations. Tingling or numbness, excessive sweating, nausea, dizziness, and tremors can also occur.

Some panic attacks are triggered by specific situations, such as crossing a bridge or being in a crowded supermarket. A person can be calm or anxious when the upswing in panic symptoms begins. The attack usually begins abruptly and builds rapidly to a peak, and the whole miserable experience usually lasts less than half an hour. These panic attacks may lead to worrying about them happening again or avoiding situations in which they have occurred.

Panic attacks are common. At least 30% of all adults have experienced at least one. They can occur as isolated experiences in healthy adults. Some people even awaken at night with nocturnal attacks. Women are more often affected than men. It is believed the number of males who struggle with panic disorder is much higher because many don't report it to their doctors. In addition, panic attacks often co-exist with depression.

Separation anxiety

Separation anxiety occurs when a person becomes anxious when separated from a parent or other attachment figure. Separation anxiety affects both children and adults.

Affected children fear what might happen to an important person in their lives (usually parents), so they resist being alone. They imagine that the important person will die or become lost (or that they will). Even the thought of separation can cause anxiety, nightmares, vomiting spells, or other physical complaints. They may be reluctant to attend school or sleep away from home or even in their own beds.

Separation anxiety may begin with an event such as moving to a new house or school, a medical procedure, or the loss of a valuable friend, pet, or parent. Symptoms often show up as refusal to go to school. Younger children may show reluctance at being left with a sitter or at daycare. Children may use physical complaints, imagined or otherwise, as justification for staying home with parents. Children with separation anxiety often have parents who suffer with an adult form. As with most anxiety disorders, there is a strong genetic component.

Adults, too, may fear that something horrible will happen to an important attachment figure – perhaps a spouse or even a child. As a result, they are reluctant to leave home or any place of safety. They may fear sleeping alone and experience nightmares about separation. When apart from the principal attachment figure, they may need to telephone or otherwise touch base several times a day. Some may try to ensure safety by setting a routine of following the other person.

Specific phobias

People with specific phobias have unwarranted fears of particular objects or situations. The most common phobias concern animals, blood, heights, airplane travel, being closed in, water, and thunderstorms. The anxiety produced by the exposure to one of these stimuli may take the form of a panic attack or of a more generalized sense of anxiety. However, it is always directed at something specific. This specific situation or thing consistently causes such immediate, irrational dread or anxiety that the person avoids it or endures it. These people can also worry about what they might do – faint, panic, lose control – if they have to confront whatever they are afraid of. Generally, the closer they are to the feared stimulus (and the more difficult it would be to escape), the worse they feel.

People can have more than one phobia. A person who is about to face one of these feared activities or objects will immediately begin to feel nervous or panicky – a condition known as "anticipatory anxiety". The degree of discomfort is often mild, however, so most people do not seek professional help. When it causes a person to avoid feared situations, anticipatory anxiety can be a major inconvenience; it can even interfere with working. People with specific phobias involving blood, injury, or injection often experience what is called a vasovagal response. This means that reduced heart rate and blood pressure actually cause the person to faint.

In the general population, a specific phobia is one of the most frequently reported anxiety disorders. Onset is usually in childhood or adolescence; animal phobias especially tend to begin early. Some start after a traumatic event, such as being bitten by an animal.

Obsessive-Compulsive Disorder (OCD)

A person with Obsessive-Compulsive Disorder carries out repetitive actions in a particular manner. Obsessions may include persistent and unwanted thoughts, urges, or images. These thoughts are intrusive and cause distress or anxiety. People with OCD might try to get rid of the obsession by performing a compulsive behaviour or ritual. An obsession focuses on the thought, whereas compulsion refers to the action. Obsessions persist even though the person may believe the unwanted thoughts, urges, or images are not real and try to resist them.

It is equally common among males and females. One third of afflicted adults had their first symptoms in childhood.

Post-Traumatic Stress Disorder (PTSD)

Post-Traumatic Stress Disorder (PTSD) can develop after a person is exposed to a severely traumatic event or many "minor" traumatic events. PTSD is triggered– either through actual experience or witnessing it. Symptoms may include flashbacks, nightmares, and severe anxiety, as well as uncontrollable thoughts about the event.

After some delay (symptoms don't usually develop immediately), the person in some way relives the traumatic event(s) and tries to avoid thinking about it or them. There are also symptoms of physiological hyper-arousal, such as an exaggerated startle response. Those with PTSD also express negative feelings such as guilt or personal responsibility. ("I should have prevented it.")

PTSD symptoms are generally grouped into four types: intrusive memories, avoidance, negative changes in thinking and mood, and changes in physical and emotional reactions. Symptoms can vary over time and from person to person. Some people respond to reminders of the event with physiological sensations (racing heart, shortness of breath) or emotional distress and may take steps to avoid the horror, by refusing to watch films or television or read accounts of similar events. Those affected by PTSD may also have persistent negative moods and gloomy thoughts, such as: "I'm useless," "The world is a mess," "I can't believe anyone," etc. Some people lose interest in meaningful activities and feel detached. Others may experience amnesia for some aspects of the trauma or become numb and feel unable to love or experience joy. Some experience symptoms of irritability, excessive vigilance, trouble concentrating, or insomnia.

The overall lifetime prevalence of PTSD is estimated at about 9% of the population. It is also estimated that 30% of first responders will develop PTSD. Females are more likely to be afflicted than males. Rape is a very common trigger of PTSD. Sixty-five percent of males and 46% of females who are raped will develop the disorder. Childhood sexual abuse is a strong predictor of lifetime likelihood for developing PTSD.

PTSD sufferers are encouraged to seek help. Many believe that their condition will "just go away," but unfortunately, the reverse is true: The longer the condition remains, the more entrenched it becomes, and the more difficult it is to resolve.

Hangover anxiety

It is common to experience hangover anxiety or "hangxiety" with a hangover. A 2019 study found that "hangxiety" is not an isolated phenomenon, and its intensity varies. Shyer people felt higher levels of anxiety the day after drinking than people who had a lower baseline of shyness. It's believed that the rebound effects are felt more intensely by shy people because their amygdala (the part of the brain that processes emotion) is more active to begin with. They are more likely to ruminate on the previous night's actions.

Marijuana-related anxiety

Ten percent of those who have Cannabis Use Disorder (CUD) or problematic marijuana use also suffer from Social Anxiety Disorder (SAD).

Research on experiences with marijuana and anxiety shows marijuana can cause panic attacks and prolonged issues with anxiety. In a recent online poll conducted, 40% of those who tried marijuana said marijuana contributed to their struggle with an anxiety disorder. Sixteen percent said their anxiety problems resulted directly from marijuana use. As well, 72% of those that had a negative experience with marijuana said marijuana contributed to their struggle with anxiety.

Not everyone experiences anxiety the same way. It is possible to experience more than one type of anxiety. The more anxiety you experience, the harder life can feel.

CHAPTER 3

What causes anxiety?

The causes of anxiety are different for everyone. Sometimes a difficult time in your life can trigger anxiety; sometimes it is caused by a combination of things that have built up over time; and sometimes, there is just no obvious cause at all.

Sometimes the symptoms you are experiencing are masquerading as anxiety, but are in fact something else. Certain situations may trigger anxiety from the past, causing us to re-live rather than live our lives. Anxiety also can be a behaviour we learn from our parents or life experiences.

The truth is that the causes of anxiety disorders aren't fully understood. While people with anxiety disorders regularly have a genetic predisposition towards them, physical factors such as diet or an imbalance of hormones and chemical messengers (i.e. neurotransmitters) in areas of the brain also can play an important role. Life experiences such as traumatic events appear to trigger anxiety disorders in people who are already prone to anxiety.

The following are some common contributing factors to anxiety.

Stress

Everyone knows that stress affects us negatively, but chronic stress also physically changes the brain. Research done at the University of California, Berkeley shows that chronic stress changes the production of myelin (the fatty substance that surrounds nerve cells to insulate them and increase the rate which electrical impulses can travel), which in turn disrupts communication patterns within the brain. Stress also influences the production of neurotransmitters, which play a key role in anxiety. A big event or a build-up of smaller stressful life situations may trigger excessive anxiety – for example a death in the family, work stress, or ongoing worry about finances.

Trauma

People who have endured abuse or trauma or have witnessed traumatic events are at higher risk of developing an anxiety disorder at some point in life.

Serious health events and chronic illness

Having a health condition or serious illness can cause significant worry about issues such as your treatment and your future. A sudden or unexpected health event – such as a heart attack or stroke, diagnosis of cancer, or other serious illness or injury – can change your life in many ways. Feelings of shock, anger, grief, loss, and sadness are common. These feelings usually pass with time, however, if they cause ongoing stress, you may be at greater risk of developing depression and anxiety. Similarly, if you live with a chronic illness (e.g., heart disease, diabetes, arthritis, or asthma), you are also at a greater risk of developing depression and anxiety.

Alcohol and drug use

Drug and alcohol use can both lead to and result from anxiety. Anxiety can be a drug side effect. It is very common, for men in particular, to try to mask or block out the symptoms of anxiety by using alcohol or drugs, which only makes the symptoms worse. Withdrawal from alcohol or drugs also can cause anxiety.

Medical conditions related to ageing

In addition to psychological causes, medical disorders common in older adults can be directly responsible for anxiety. These include heart disease, neurological illness, thyroid, and other hormone problems.

But not all symptoms that look like anxiety are in fact anxiety.

Is it anxiety or is it something else?

Anxiety can be due to an underlying medical condition, and this is something to consider if you have a sudden occurrence of anxiety that seems unrelated to life events and you don't have a previous history of anxiety and/or have any blood relatives (such as a parent or sibling) with an anxiety disorder.

It's surprising just how many medical conditions can cause anxiety symptoms. Many people dealing with a medical issue may experience anxiety as a result.

A few medical conditions are explained next.

Blood sugar imbalance

Anyone who is experiencing chronic anxiety needs to first look at their blood sugar levels. Unstable blood sugar and anxiety symptoms are almost identical. Two of the most common blood sugar conditions are hypoglycemia and insulin resistance.

Hypoglycemia

The standard North American diet of sugar and carbs is literally a recipe for chronic anxiety. Daily spikes in blood sugar trigger constant snacking and anxiety-like symptoms.

In hypoglycemia, there's a spike in blood sugar and then a major drop after the pancreas reacts by producing insulin. Hypoglycemia literally means "low sugar". When this happens, the brain and body start to panic because their resource (sugar) needed for energy is getting low. The brain needs more energy than any other organ in the body. It sends an SOS message to the adrenals, which release the stress hormone cortisol. The body goes into a fight-or-flight state. In this state we feel anxiety symptoms like heart palpitations, panic, fear, shakes, and dizziness.

In a 2018 case study done by M. Aucoin and S. Bhardwaj (Canadian College of Naturopathic Medicine), a link between diet that caused hypoglycemia and anxiety was discovered. A 15-year-old female presented with severe anxiety, which included excessive worry, discomfort in her stomach, and heart palpitations that impacted her ability to function. Her anxiety was so severe she missed school regularly.

Her formal diagnosis was generalized anxiety disorder. She rated her anxiety as eight out of ten.

Researchers found that her diet and eating habits were the typical, standard North American diet of high carbohydrates and little fat – including granola bars, bagels, orange juice, pastas, and constant snacking. When she switched to a high-protein and a higher fat diet, her symptoms went to a four out of ten, and she had higher energy, fewer stomach aches, and a greater ability to concentrate. She reported that if she went back to her previous diet, her anxiety immediately returned.

Insulin resistance

Every time you eat carbohydrates, the body breaks them down into glucose as your body digests them. Glucose is released into the blood stream, causing a rise in blood sugar. The pancreas responds by releasing insulin to balance the spike in blood sugar. If blood glucose levels remain too high (e.g. from eating carbohydrates throughout the day), over time the cells stop responding to insulin. Excess blood sugar stays floating around and doing all types of damage, especially to the brain.

Insulin resistance alters the production of dopamine (a neurotransmitter) and affects the way neurons fire in the brain and the communication between brain cells. A study done by the Joslin Diabetes Center found a direct link between the brain and behavioural disorders.

Intermittent fasting can help heal insulin resistance. It has healing benefits for both the mind and the body. Canadian nephrologist, Dr. Jason Fung, is an excellent source of information on intermittent fasting. He has written several books and has many free podcasts that explain intermittent fasting in detail. Intermittent fasting can be a major game changer.

Nutrient deficiencies and anxiety

When someone is experiencing chronic anxiety, nutritional deficiencies aren't the first thing that come to mind, but they should be. Our bodies need a specific amount of nutrients that work together in a sophisticated symphony with each other. Deficiencies or incorrect ratios of nutrients often manifest as anxiety-like symptoms.

Here are a few examples:

Magnesium is a mineral that supports 300 biochemical reactions in the body. Magnesium is essential for proper functioning of the nervous system and neurotransmitter activity. It is closely tied to gamma aminobutyric acid (GABA) production, and low levels of this contribute to anxiety.

Zinc also plays a vital role in neurotransmitter and central nervous system functioning. Studies show that significantly low zinc levels can trigger anxiety. Zinc supplementation has been shown to reduce symptoms of anxiety.

Vitamin D is actually a hormone rather than a vitamin; it is required to absorb calcium from the gut into the bloodstream. Vitamin D is connected to almost every system in the body. It plays a key role in anxiety and many other psychiatric disorders.

Vitamin D is mostly produced in the skin in response to sunlight and is also absorbed from food eaten (about 10% of vitamin D is absorbed this way) as part of a healthy, balanced diet. It's estimated that up to 85% of us are not getting enough. That's epidemic proportions, and a reason to be conscious about spending some time in the sun.

Iron is found in every cell of the human body. Its role is to carry oxygen to different organs in the body, which is why low levels lead to tiredness and irritability. Iron is also key in the synthesis of the neurotransmitter serotonin. People with anxiety disorders have significantly lower levels of iron.

Omega-3 fatty acids cannot be made by the body, so they must be found in food. Unfortunately, we have been told to fear fats and our brains have paid the price. The brain is primarily made up of fat and needs omega-3's for cognitive and nervous system function. People with the most severe anxiety have the lowest levels of omega-3 fatty acids.

Microbiome imbalance

Our entire gastrointestinal tract is filled with various bacteria, fungi and other micro-organisms. We have more gut bacteria than human genes. Diet, sleep, and stress all influence our gastrointestinal microbiome.

Seventy percent of neurotransmitters like serotonin are made in the gut and then sent through to the brain via the gut-brain axis. Our gut-brain axis is a two-way communication centre between the gut and the brain. These gut bacteria determine not only our overall health, but also our thoughts and mood.

When we have an imbalance of microbes (meaning more "bad" microbes than "good" ones), all types of psychiatric disorders can happen from anxiety to depression and mood disorders.

A ground-breaking study done at University College Cork, Ireland was the first to make a connection between microbes and a specific molecule called microRNA in the amygdala and prefrontal cortex of the brain. Researchers took two groups of mice and measured their micro RNA levels in the amygdala and pre-frontal cortex. The levels were virtually the same in both groups. One group had gut microbes removed and the other group was untreated. In the microbe-free mice, researchers found microRNAs in the amygdala and microRNA's in the prefrontal cortex were changed compared to the untreated mice. When researchers added gut bacteria and microbes back into the microbe-free mice, the levels normalized. This was the first time a study showed that the gut physically changed the brain.

This is pretty mind blowing and a reason that balancing the microbes in our gut should be a major part of any mental health treatment.

Remember: It is important to consult your doctor and discuss your health and any symptoms you are experiencing.

Is your past controlling your anxiety?

We all replay events in our heads that can cause us to feel stressed or regretful, but some of us get stuck on a cycle of repeat that doesn't allow us to move on. This happens in many ways – both through explicit memories of actual events and also through implicit memories (things that we don't necessarily remember consciously but that have impacted our thoughts, feelings, and behaviours).

Many present situations can trigger tensions from our past. Our anxiety can be elevated by experiences that remind us of old ways we felt about ourselves or our circumstances. This is one of the main reasons that making sense of our past can be a powerful tool to under-stand and overcome anxiety in the present. It may seem like our stress about work or our worries about our relationships are entirely based on current conditions, but the ways we experience, react, feel, and torture ourselves in these scenarios are often reflections of old, unresolved feel-ings that have been stirred up.

Most of us have one of two ways of dealing with the past. Some of us try to bury it away. Our attitude is whatever happened "happened"; we can't change it, so we should just let it go. Others of us seem to get stuck in their history and are deeply triggered by memories or become overwhelmed by old feelings. These people struggle to let the past go. Research shows us that neither of these attitudes is particularly adaptive or beneficial to our personal development. Although these approaches to the past may seem entirely contradictory, they lead to the same ultimate outcome. If we avoid facing the past, we fail to recognize the many, often limiting, ways it is influencing our present. On the other hand, if we over-identify with and ruminate on our childhood experiences, we still find ourselves being ruled by these events. In both cases, we are failing to differentiate and live our lives on our own terms.

Research shows that in order to free ourselves from the past, form healthier relationships, and show up today as the people we want to be, we have to make sense and feel the full pain of our story. When we fail to face unresolved pain from our childhood, we have many, often unconscious, ways of repeating it. These repetitive patterns are not intentional or thought out. It may not consciously feel like the big and small traumas from our early lives are dictating our actions, but they come out in ways we don't realize – for example, in the partners we choose, critical attitudes we have toward ourselves, and the dynamics we create with our children. Events from our present day lives trigger implicit memories that are often painful and cause us to react rather than act in our own best interest. In this sense, we're often re-living rather than living our lives.

Here are some of the ways we re-live rather than live our lives:

Repeat

One of the ways that we carry our past into the present is by repeating behaviours and taking on characteristics of important figures from our early lives. Of course, this can be a good thing when we are adopting ways of being that we value and respect. However, as human beings, we have a tendency to over-identify with the negative traits of our parents or early caretakers. We struggle to see ourselves in a different light from the people who originally cared for us. On an unconscious level, we take on our parents' traits in an effort to preserve an idealized image of them.

While it may seem counterintuitive, it can feel painful or threatening to separate ourselves from our parents by seeing them realistically, including all the ways they were limited and hurt us. Instead, we identify with our parents and take on their qualities. For example, if we had an especially elusive or inward parent, we may find ourselves feeling unavailable to our loved ones or pulling away from relationships when they get too close. If we had a parent who worried excessively and intruded on us, we may find ourselves feeling the same way toward our children and acting in ways that are invasive or overbearing.

React

The opposite side of the same coin comes when we rebel against our parents' way of being. It is healthy and wise to identify traits we don't like in our early caretakers and to choose to be different in these ways. However, we sometimes are so determined to be different from our family of origin that we overcompensate or distort our natural way of being. For example, if we hated the way our parents did not get along; we may grow up writing off relationships or love in general. We may vow to never get "too serious" with someone or trust anyone on a deep level.

Or, if we felt deprived as kids, we may try to make up for it by overindulging or spoiling our own children. We may project onto our kids that they feel like we did when we were young, and therefore, react to them in ways that are not in line with their actual wants and needs. In each of these cases, we are still seeing the present through a filter of our past and failing to separate ourselves from our history. We are not allowing ourselves to fully realize who we really are and what we really want.

Re-create

Another way we fail to step out from the shadows of our past is by re-creating environments and dynamics that are similar to those we experienced growing up. This pattern can be tricky to identify, but here are some common examples: we may find ourselves somehow dating or marrying people who treat us in ways that are similar to how we were treated as kids; if we grew up with a parent who made us feel small or insignificant, we may find ourselves attracted to partners who are more dismissive; or if we had a parent who fawned over us, we may only feel drawn to people who build us up or offer us all their attention.

Another way we re-create past dynamics is by distorting figures in our lives and projecting traits or reactions onto them that come from our history. For instance, if we had an untrustworthy, flaky, or dismissive person in our early lives, we may consistently feel that we are being deceived as adults. We may assume our partner is pulling away or cheating on us, even when there are no real signs that this is the case.

Lastly, we may even unconsciously provoke people in our lives to react to us in ways that are familiar, even though they were painful. If we were seen as babyish or incompetent as kids, for instance, we may find ourselves acting more helpless or needy with our partner. If we had a parent who lost his or her temper, we may try to provoke that same reaction from the people we are closest to in our adult lives by insulting them or trying to push their buttons.

Repeating, reacting and re-creating patterns of behaviour may lead to unpleasant, even devastating outcomes, but they also help us maintain habitual, old, often negative ways of feeling about ourselves. Even if we are hundreds of kilometres and many years away from our childhood environment, these patterns allow us to remain in these familiar environments on a psychological and emotional level. This lack of differentiation can cause us to feel bonded to our early caretakers in ways that limit us. This illusion of connection may have felt like a lifesaving adaptation when we were little and needed these people for our very survival, but as adults, these patterns are no longer adaptive and hurt us in our ability to become who we want to be.

To the extent that we don't recognize and separate from these destructive adaptations, we fail to live our own lives. The good news is that by creating a coherent narrative of what happened to us, we can separate from unfavourable overlays of our past and become the people we want to be. When we start this journey to better know our own story, we open ourselves up to new possibilities and liberate ourselves to make real change and create a better future.

Does anxiety come from nature or nurture?

Research shows that anxiety disorders tend to run in families. However, it isn't entirely clear how much of this may be due to genetics (nature) and how much is due to learned behaviour (nurture). On the "nature" side, genetics could cause a person to have an overactive amygdala, which may cause a heightened fear response, and increased anxiety in social situations.

However, research also shows that some people who suffer from anxiety grew up in very anxious families. Parents may have suffered from generalized anxiety, social anxiety, agoraphobia, panic disorder, Obsessive-Compulsive Disorder (OCD), and/or Post-Traumatic Stress Disorder (PTSD). Often, these parents were never formally diagnosed with a mental health disorder. It is only after the fact, when a person is an adult, that they can recognize and understand how anxious their parents were and how it has affected their mental health, both during childhood and into adulthood.

It is extremely difficult on a child to grow up with an anxious parent, and even harder if both parents, and sometimes extended family as well, are anxious. Anxiety is a disorder characterized by constriction – it keeps people from living full and free lives and often encourages "worst-case-scenario" thinking. Here are some of the things that parents with anxiety may teach their kids, implicitly and explicitly:

- The world is dangerous.
- Other people are not to be trusted. (This may also manifest itself as unfounded prejudices – e.g., men/women/people who are a different ethnicity are not to be trusted.)
- Unpredictability is something to be feared.
- You need to try to control everything so that you don't get hurt.
- It is easiest just to stay home and not interact with anyone.
- Don't take any risks because it would be worse to fail than not to try.

These lessons, and others, explain why so many individuals who grew up with anxious parents often end up in therapy, trying to work out their own mental health challenges. Imagine trying to approach a romantic interest when you have learned from a socially anxious parent that all people are judgmental and self-centred. Imagine trying to join your friends' white-water rafting trip when you have heard over and over throughout your life that drownings happen every day.

In general, imagine trying to live your life without fear when you have learned from childhood that fear is a totally acceptable default state of being.

Add to the mix the fact that many highly anxious parents do not perceive themselves as anxious and see their behaviour and thoughts as rooted in fact. Often, such people have a trauma history – e.g., the mother who repeatedly warns her daughter that all men are predators may have been raped as a teenager, or the dad who says that people of another ethnicity are not to be trusted may be a first-generation immigrant who was teased by people of his new homeland.

In other cases, anxious parents may feel that their anxiety is a positive thing and desensitize their children to its debilitating effects. They may frame their worst-case-scenario mindset as foresight or their perfectionism as a motivating engine that keeps them on track and has a positive impact on their academic and career success. Some OCD or hoarding parents completely deny their behaviour, which can be confusing for their children.

There are many known and unknown causes of anxiety. Various medical issues can disguise themselves as anxiety and can be relieved through medical intervention. Always check with your doctor to eliminate any medical reasons for your anxiety symptoms.

CHAPTER 4

We are all affected by anxiety

The truth is we are all affected by anxiety. We experience it as children, teenagers, and adults in our relationships and in our workplaces. We are not only affected by our own anxiety. Most people are, or have been, affected by a life partner, friend, supervisor, or co-worker who is coping with anxiety.

There has been a long-standing belief that women are more prone to anxiety than men, but a closer look at the research shows that this belief is not scientifically supported.

Anxiety has become the number one mental health issue in North America. It is estimated that:

Anxiety currently affects about one in 13 people – a staggering 7.3 percent of the world population.

Approximately 12 percent of Canadians and 18 percent of Americans (nearly 40 million adults between the ages of 18 to 54) are affected by anxiety disorders.

These groups are affected by anxiety for specific reasons:

Employees

A recent survey showed 41 percent of employees from a range of industries reported high levels of anxiety in the workplace. The University of Toronto, Scarborough and Rotman School of Management found that high levels of emotional exhaustion that come from workplace anxiety can directly lead to lower job performance.

College students

Another report found that more than half of college students sought help for their anxiety issues. Research has found that anxiety can impede learning, which often leads to lower academic achievement and performance.

Gay, bisexual, and transgender people

Almost half of gay, lesbian, bisexual, transgender and gender diverse, and intersex (LGBTI) people hide or don't share their sexuality, gender identity, or intersex status because they fear violence or discrimination. However, young gay people aged 16 to 24 are more likely to do so than any other age group.

Gay, bisexual, and transgender people are much more likely to experience depression and anxiety than the broader population. They are also at a higher risk of suicide and self-harm. Among LGBTI populations, research clearly indicates that discrimination, abuse (both verbal and physical), exclusion, and prejudice are key contributors to the increased rates of depression, anxiety, and self-harm.

Compared to heterosexual people, gay and bisexual people are more likely to experience depression and anxiety conditions.

Many gay men living with HIV have lost relationships, social support networks, careers, earning capacity, and a sense of future. These multiple losses may make them more likely to develop depression and may also compound symptoms. More than 50 percent of people living with HIV report having depression or anxiety.

Aboriginal people

Depression and anxiety affects many Aboriginal people, for a whole range of reasons. These could relate to difficult situations involving inadequate housing, low income, or unemployment and compound the generations of trauma, grief, and loss Aboriginal people have experienced. Sometimes, people don't know how to describe what they are experiencing. Often, they don't want to be around family and friends.

Many Aboriginal people in Canada acutely feel racism. In a 2005 report, 38% of study participants experienced at least one instance of racism in the past 12 months.

Young adults

Depression and anxiety are among the most common mental health conditions experienced by young people. One in seven people aged between 16 and 24 experience depression or anxiety each year. Often, the symptoms aren't recognized, and therefore, young people don't get the help they need. Sometimes, the signs are ignored or passed off as "just part of growing up".

New parents

About 16 percent of all new mothers and 5 percent of new fathers develop postnatal depression in the year after having a baby. Anxiety conditions are likely to be at least as common.

Statistics show that depression and anxiety may be more common for those parents who: have been depressed before; have less practical, emotional, or social support; feel the burden of financial stress; experience a difficult birth; have current or past experiences with drugs or alcohol; have a sick baby; have significant life and relationship difficulties – past and present; or find the reality of parenting is different from their expectations.

Older men and women

Depression and anxiety in older people can happen for different reasons, such as dealing with a physical illness or personal loss. But it is important to remember that depression and anxiety are not a normal part of ageing or a weakness of character. It is a health issue, just like any other.

Older people may be more at risk of depression and/or anxiety due to: an increase in physical health problems/conditions (e.g., cancer, cardiovascular disease, dementia, stroke, chronic pain, side-effects from medications); losses (e.g., relationships, independence, work and income, self-worth, mobility and flexibility); social isolation; and significant change in living arrangements (e.g., moving from living independently to a care facility, or admission to hospital.

Unemployed people

Declining economy and unexpected income loss can have a massive financial and emotional impact on many people. Loss of your job, significant investment losses, and/or loss of retirement income are all contributors to anxiety.

For some, financial loss may mean seeking income support. For others, it could mean revising retirement plans or cutting down on household spending. Regardless of the circumstances, most people feel understandably distressed in the face of unexpected events that involve significant loss and change. In some cases, this reaction may be similar to grief.

Health and chronic illness

People who suffer from heart attack, stroke, diagnosis of cancer, or other serious illness or injury often experience feelings of shock, anger, grief, loss, and sadness and may be at higher risk of developing depression and anxiety.

Similarly, people who suffer from a chronic illness (e.g. heart disease, diabetes, arthritis, or asthma), are also at greater risk of developing depression and anxiety. Less common chronic physical illnesses that can also be associated with depression include: chronic pain, Parkinson's disease, and Chronic Fatigue Syndrome.

What age group is most affected by anxiety?

A 2018 survey was conducted by the American Psychiatric Association (APA) to determine anxiety levels in different age groups. They found that Millennials (ages 20 to 37) were most anxious overall, followed by Baby Boomers (ages 54 to 72), and then Generation Z's (ages 38 to 53).

Anxiety disorders are the most common disorders in children and youth. The average age of onset for anxiety disorders is 11 years old. Anxiety may increase with age.

Is there such a thing as an anxious personality?

At its basic level, personality refers to who a person is – his/her thoughts, feelings, behaviours, and patterns of interpreting the world. Many things influence the development of personality, and personality is fluid; it changes over time.

There are numerous personality types. One well-known way to test and classify personality types is the "Type A/B/C/D" model. It is almost universally accepted that each of these types is associated with given traits that help define one's personality.

Type A personality: are the people characterized as driven and achievement-oriented. They are competitive and can be rather intense and high strung. They set lofty goals, and they put high demands and expectations on themselves to achieve them.

Type B personality: are more relaxed and laid back people than their Type A counterparts. They can be procrastinators; they are patient, creative, and big-picture thinkers, and sometimes they are people-oriented.

Type C personality: are detail-oriented and perfectionistic people. They tend not to be very assertive, and they generally fear criticism.

Type D personality: are people who tend to feel easily distressed and fear rejection. They can be rather pessimistic, as well – always assuming that they are not good enough and will be shunned.

If you look at each personality type, they all have the potential for anxiety. Type A's are susceptible to stress, worry, and fear of failure. Type B's are at risk for the anxiety that comes when deadlines loom and go unmet. Depending on the situation, big-picture thinkers can sometimes worry about the future. Type C's can experience social anxiety, and Type D's are prone to stress and pessimism and are at risk of generalized anxiety disorder.

Most people are a mix of personality types. Absolutely everyone has aspects of their personality that can contribute to the development of anxiety. This means that if you have anxiety, you are not flawed; you are merely being human. Interestingly, not everyone suffers from anxiety.

The reason that not everyone has anxiety is complicated, but a significant portion of it has to do with the fact that some people have strategies to keep anxiety at bay. They practice self-care. They have support systems. They have tools in their toolboxes to use to reduce anxiety.

In addition, quite a bit has to do with brain chemistry. Chemical reactions, neurotransmitter behaviour, and hormonal activity can sometimes be at the root of anxiety, no matter what your personality type is.

Gender and Anxiety

Society's behaviour rules for males and females (i.e., gender roles: masculine and feminine) may affect differences in who may suffer from anxiety and who will report it.

From childhood, boys are generally encouraged to confront feared objects, resulting in greater exposure and extinction of fear responses compared to girls. Gender differences in the division of work, socio-economic status, and social roles may leave women more vulnerable to anxiety disorders than men. Women are more exposed to certain potentially traumatic events such as sexual trauma and domestic abuse, as well as relationship stressors.

Women are more likely to report prior symptoms of anxiety than men. Often boys learn to suffer in silence because they are told to "suck it up" or "take it like a man".

Sex and Anxiety

According to various studies, females are almost twice as likely as males to experience most types of anxiety disorders. The question is: Why? As with all things related to mental health, there are likely a lot of factors involved. A new study of male and female mice has identified one part of the brain that may influence why females are more prone to anxiety than males, and it could change how we treat it.

The scientists behind this study were surprised to find what they did. They were looking at a part of the brain called the locus coeruleus, which is found in human and mice brains. The locus coeruleus is responsible for a lot of things, but one of its biggest responsibilities is producing a hormone called norepinephrine (medical terminology has changed over time, adrenalin is now referred to as epinephrine and noradrenalin is now referred to as norepinephrine). A deficiency of norepinephrine is linked to depression, anxiety, and sleep problems.

An entire class of antidepressants, Serotonin-Norepinephrine Reuptake Inhibitors (SNRIs), is designed to raise deficient levels of it.

When the scientists looked at the locus coeruleus, they discovered something very odd. The locus coeruleus in the brains of female mice looks very different compared to the brains of male mice. For one, it has much, much more of a receptor called PTGER3, which manages the body's stress responses. Second, other studies show it contains more genes that have been linked to depression.

Why does this difference matter? Well, during the experiment, the scientists gave the mice a standard medicine that was supposed to calm them down after a stressful experience, and only the female mice responded – because the drug was designed to interact with PTGER3.

In plain English, these brain differences mean that some anxiety drugs will probably work for females and not males, and vice versa. This fact is tremendously important for everyone currently on anxiety medications – particularly females.

Of course, we don't yet know if this difference is the same in human brains as it is in mice; that will be the next stage of the research. But if it is, it could be game changing. It would explain why females are more prone to suffer from anxiety, which could help to reduce stigma. It would also revolutionize how we treat anxiety and depression because scientists would start to investigate treatments based on sex.

The reason we are just finding this out now is because of sexual bias in medicine. For a very long time, **scientists only used males** – male mice, male rats, and male humans – in their experiments, thinking this would provide an accurate result that applied to everybody. But it turns out (surprise!) that female biology can be radically different. Sexual bias can be attributed to the fact that research is still such a heavily male-dominated field. However, as science continues to see more diversity, our scientific findings will likely be better off for it, as well.

The locus coeruleus study results reaffirm why it is so important to include both sexes in tests because the research might uncover some unexpected contrasts that can be critical in developing new medicines or other ways to help people. Following this research, there is also the possibility of new anti-anxiety medication specifically tailored for both female and male brain structures. All of this is far in the future, but for now, this study serves as proof positive that sexual equality in the lab is necessary.

There are many factors that contribute to anxiety including gender roles, life situations, age, sex and personality. It is important to remember that you are not alone if you suffer from anxiety.

CHAPTER 5

Your brain, memory, and neuroplasticity

There can be many contributing factors to anxiety beyond your past, upbringing, sex or gender. For instance, your brain's tendency to generalize can be the starting point of anxiety. Ruminating over the past further entrenches anxious feelings. However, our memories are not perfect and you may be basing your beliefs and anxious responses on imperfect information.

It has only been in the past 150 years that we have really known anything about the brain and most of this has been learned in the last 30 years. Brain research often uses brain-scanning techniques such as electroencephalography, positron emission tomography, magneto encephalography, computed tomography and tensor imaging. As a result of these amazing advances, we are able to understand more of how the brain operates and impacts our behaviour.

One of the most fundamental concepts learned has been how individual neurons interact. Your brain is malleable and is constantly rewiring itself (scientists now refer to the brain's ability to rewire itself as *neuroplasticity*). Scientists once believed that you were born with a certain number of brain cells, after which it was all downhill, but now we realize that new brain cells are being created all the time in a process called neurogenesis. In fact, your brain is so eager to make new connections that, on average, one million neural connections are made for every second of your life.

But how does your brain know what connections to make, and what is the process that allows this to happen? The answer is referred to as Hebb's Law.

Hebb's Law

A psychologist named Donald Hebb was fascinated with how children who had brain surgery that involved removing portions of the brain appeared to be able to regain much, or all, of their mental abilities. In 1949, Hebb made the landmark discovery that the brain can rewire itself to compensate for damage. He came up with a theory known as Hebb's Law. Simply put: **Neurons that fire together, wire together.**

This means that if your brain fires off two neurons – or two networks of neurons at the same time – they will begin to become wired together. For example, think of the Nike logo, the big check mark. It may make you think of the phrase "Just do it". The two neural networks involved in these concepts have gotten to know each other. It is almost as if they are reaching out and shaking hands with each other.

Your brain's tendency to generalize

Early scientists discovered that the brain tends to generalize. It likes to link up situations and contexts that are different. Russian physiologist Ivan Pavlov understood this principle when he paired the ringing of a bell to the feeding of his dogs. After a while, the ringing of a bell would make the dogs salivate whether or not they were being fed at that time. This is known as classical conditioning, which means that the stimulus – a bell in this case – automatically produces the response (the salivation).

This is how phobias develop. For example, a person has a bad experience in one elevator, and they generalize it to all elevators. If someone has been afraid in one elevator, how does that person know to be afraid in another one? The answer is generalization, and generalization is a by-product of the process explained by Hebb's Law.

The more links and associations you have with a problem, the stronger it is. When you have a fear of all elevators, that fear is much stronger than a fear of one particular elevator.

The brain doesn't only generalize according to context; it also generalizes according to emotional state (happiness, anger, sadness, panic etc.) because the brain will sort for "like-minded states". State-dependent memory is the brain's tendency to make neuro associations and link similar states together.

Ultimately, if stimulus-driven neurons fire together enough times, they will always fire together. They will become part of one network. If they shake hands enough times, they become such firm friends that they never let go. Here are some more examples of Hebb's Law in practice:

You meet a man named Roger. You see his face, and that picture is stored in a network of neurons in your visual cortex. You hear his voice, and that sound is stored in a separate set of neurons in your auditory cortex. You learn various autobiographical facts about him, which are stored elsewhere in your brain. All these networks become linked to form a larger network representing "Roger". When you think of "Roger", you see his face, hear his voice, recall that he lives in Vancouver, and so on.

You are also friends with Stella, and you build a mental representation of her as well held in a network of neurons in your brain labeled "Stella". Roger and Stella meet, begin dating, and become inseparable. Whenever you see Roger, you see Stella. Whenever you meet with Stella, Roger is there. As a result, your brain links the network or neurons representing Roger to the network of neurons representing Stella to create a combined network representing "Roger-and-Stella". After a period of time, your brain will begin to think of Roger and Stella as one unit, and soon you will be unable to think of one without the other.

Here is another example of Hebb's Law. During show and tell at school, you become nervous. Your presentation at college makes you extremely nervous. You have to give a presentation at your first job and are nervous to the point of panic. At some point in this process, your brain has wired together "give-presentation" and "nervous" to create one mental circuit "give-presentation = nervous".

Suppose you are standing next to someone at the bus stop and that person nudges you. Now you're watching out for that person. You're aware of that person; you have a temporary sensitive awareness.

If you don't see that person for a month after you get off the bus, you forget the encounter and probably won't recognize that person if you see him/her again. But suppose the person nudged you twice or even three times at the bus stop. You would really notice him or her. If the person even leans in your direction when you see them again, you would react. This is what your neurons do. When two neurons fire at the same time, the wiring doesn't change, but the neurons do become more sensitive to each other from that very first time they fire, creating a temporary sensitivity that lasts for about a day or two. This is called *long term potentiation*. The more times the neurons fire, the more permanent the long-term potentiation becomes, and the less energy it takes to maintain long term potentiation. As long-term potentiation continues, it leads to a permanent rewiring, which is Hebb's Law.

Now, suppose you were on the bus and a person nudged you and made a snide comment, which really made you angry. You might walk away, but you would be replaying the encounter and thinking of different ways you could or should have responded. Suppose you then see a friend, and you tell them about the incident and get all worked up again. Then you go home at night and your daughter asks you, "How was your day?" You likely will say, "It started off really messed up because of this guy on the bus..."

Humans tend to overthink things. We worry about what might happen in the future, we ruminate over things that have happened in the past. We dwell on past mistakes. Ruminating on thoughts impacts on our neural pathways.

Quantum zeno effect

The quantum zeno effect is a principle in quantum physics that states that observing the rate of decay of a particle or system slows down the decay. In other words, the process of observation stabilizes the system – a case of "a watched pot never boils". This isn't just a theory; it has been tested in the laboratory. Physicists have looked at atomic particles and found that by observing it and checking on it, it becomes stabilized longer than an atomic particle that isn't being constantly observed.

The quantum zeno effect also applies to thought in general and neural networks in particular. The more we put our attention on something, the more it tends to persist.

Returning to the bus stop example: The quantum zeno effect is different than long term potentiation because the effect doesn't have to be about the actual person nudging you; it can be just remembering what happened, replaying it, thinking about it, imagining it, talking to yourself about it, or beating yourself up because you didn't say anything to the person. All these reactions reinforce the neuronal link between the bus, the person, and the negative emotion because just replaying incidents, good or bad, in the imagination also wires them together.

What is amazing is that it works the other way as well. Just by imagining what you want to happen or how you want to be, begins to re-wire your neural pathways.

For example, when someone says, "I have this problem, and it's terrible, and it happens all the time." She is stabilizing the problem. If she wanted to get rid of the problem, all she would really have to do is stop thinking about it. This may sound ridiculous and way too easy, but if a person stopped thinking about a particular problem and started thinking about what she wanted instead, that problem would disappear by itself.

Many problems are being stabilized through constant attention. People ruminate in many ways about how they feel and think about their problems, and they worry that they will never be able to change them. The quantum zeno effect is played out in countless therapy and coaching sessions across the globe. The important point is that research really does back up the idea that you get what you focus on. This fact gives you a great reason to interrupt your story by using a **pattern-interrupt** to begin to break the quantum zeno effect.

You will learn more about how to interrupt your thoughts by using a number of methods covered in the Toolkit section. The more the pattern is interrupted, the more successful you will be.

In order to unlearn old habituated patterns and create new ones, it is crucial to understand how your brain, memories, and neuroplasticity work and how to work with them to make lasting changes.

We want to know why we are anxious

We all seek understanding, meaning, wisdom, and knowledge. We want to know why we are here. We crave purpose. For many of us, we navigate life trying to make sense of who we are. We are trying to find ourselves.

Some people get fixated with a need to know "why" they feel anxious. They seek to find a situation, reason, or person to blame for their anxiety. They believe if they just knew "why", their anxiety would easily just melt away. Unfortunately, that's not the case.

Even if we do understand the "why", people remain anxious; "why" changes nothing. Usually there is not one single cause for a problem, but a multitude of causes. The focus of therapy should not be "why", but instead: How do I live fully in the present moment?

Another term for living fully in the moment is "mindfulness". You will learn how to practice mindfulness and be able to practice it by using the audio recording that you downloaded when you started reading this book.

Simply knowing the exact cause of anxiety will not remove it. You have to do the work to remove anxiety.

We can't change the past

The reality is that while we can process the past forever, we will never be able to change it. One of Freud's central ideas was that we could visit past memories to find the cause of today's issue. He thought we could resolve that past problem through a series of different processes and then experience life more fully in the present. It made for a great theory in the early 1900s but the evidence shows us that memory isn't particularly accurate or even useful in many cases. The next chapter gives an understanding of how memory actually works and will clarify this for you.

So many therapies focus on the person's past – what they believe they did wrong, regrets and shame they continually carry – and trying to undo past mistakes. By carrying the past into the present moment, they are still living in the past.

Conversely, there are those who place too much emphasis on the future. They miss living in the present moment and feel out of control. You will learn not only how to master your thoughts, but how to live in a place of moment-to-moment awareness.

By using the techniques explained in *The Anxiety Fix* you don't have to rehash the past and relive painful feelings. Instead you will learn how to think in the moment and change your thought patterns right there and then.

This is the control you have over your life – your thoughts.

CHAPTER 6

Memory: Can you trust yours?

Humans dwell on the past, or what they remember as the past. Anxiety can develop and escalate from ruminating over the past. But how trustworthy is your memory?

Neuroscience provides significant insights into memories. These insights include information about memory integration, memory distribution, and memory reconsolidation. Understanding memory is vital to understanding how learning and, consequently, change takes place.

Memory consolidation is the process whereby our brains convert short-term memories into long-term ones.

Short-term memory tends to be quite limited in terms of duration and capacity. The human brain can only store short-term memories for about 30 seconds, so if you are going to remember something important, the information must be moved into long-term memory.

Attention or mindfulness

Attention is the basis of learning; learning is the basis of memory; and creating new memories is the basis of change. Without attention, it all falls apart, so it is vital to know what attention is, how to get it, and what we do with it once we have it.

There are two types of attention: intrinsic and phasic. Intrinsic attention is paying attention to all the sensory information available to us at any one time. This could also be called *mindfulness*; this state allows us to pay attention to threats as they arise without the need to maintain a constant state of fearfulness. Unfortunately, it is a state that we often lose in the modern world of cell phones, stress, and rapid-fire informational inputs.

Being aware of what is going on at any given moment, particularly being aware of feelings and emotions that we are experiencing, is the key to allowing us to change.

Paying attention to your internal mental processes, particularly what is going on in the video and audio loops of your working memory is important.

Most people are playing movies of events that have gone wrong in the past or events they are afraid will happen in the future and are basically **programming themselves for failure**.

Attention density is determined by a number of factors, the greatest being repetition. The more time we spend thinking about something – activating the emotions that fuel and are fuelled by those thoughts – the more neurons and neural networks we recruit. Attention density is important because, as Hebb's Law explains, it causes neural circuits to wire together.

When a person thinks about a problem frequently, obsesses about it, tells everyone about it, and constantly considers how it impacts her life, she is strengthening the neural pathways that are linked to the problem. This type of thinking increases the attention density associated with the problem and will wire the problem more deeply within the brain.

This is why it is crucial to understand that to deal with anxiety, you must interrupt your thought patterns. This is best achieved if you are armed with more than one way to do so.

In the same way that attention density can create or increase a problem, it can also create and solidify change, but only if you focus your attention on the outcome and on any positive changes you have already achieved. The audio recording and techniques for interrupting your anxiety explained in the Toolkit section of this book will help you reach your goal of programming yourself for success.

Learning and the reward circuit

The brain learns best when experiencing either a strong negative response, such as fear, or something very pleasurable, such as food or sex. When we get something good, such as food, our brain rewards us by releasing chemicals such as dopamine. When dopamine is released, the hippocampus is alerted that something worth learning is happening. The hippocampus responds by taking the experience that resulted in reward and encoding it into long-term memory.

To consciously learn, we have to pay attention. For example, if you are constantly checking your texts, you will not take in information that can be easily accessed later. It is dopamine that locks in your focus and attention.

Without dopamine, you can still focus if you force yourself – much like the way you focus on tasks that are mundane and boring. Dealing with taxes and boring paperwork comes to mind. It is not a lot of fun to do boring tasks, so it is easy to become distracted by texts, emails, or just random thoughts while doing them. But a dopamine rush makes accomplishing things easy. You become so engrossed that you end up saying, "Wow, I've been doing this for X number of hours? Where did the time go?"

You can use hypnosis to focus on what you are listening to as well as release dopamine. What you hear during a few minutes spent in hypnosis is laid down into the brain's long-term memory. When the movie you are watching is you rehearsing being confident and successful, your subconscious is changed, and you are changed. Change can be that easy!

To make any change permanent, the pattern must be repeated several times. That is why a change work session is an hour, not two minutes. Through repetition, you turn a new behaviour from being a mere strengthening of synapses to neurons permanently wiring together.

A lot of people have very little awareness of what is going on inside their own heads. They are unaware of the "movie" they are running in their minds. They think that they just "have" this problem or that a feeling just comes over them. They have no awareness that they are generating these feelings or that they can learn to generate different feelings.

Every time the person plays their "new movie", the neural network is reinforced, and the new way of thinking and behaving is being locked into place.

By listening to your audio recording daily, you will create new neural pathways. Your new neurons will wire together in a positive, non-anxiety invoking pattern.

Learning and sleep

Transferring learning into long-term memory is a process that continues while we sleep. In fact, sleep is vital to the laying down of long-term memories. The mechanisms underlying this process are not fully understood, but what is known is that the experiences one has throughout the day engage working memory. If the experiences are original and emotionally charged, they get stored in the hippocampus. When the person goes to sleep, the hippocampus replays the experiences and seeks to link them to other experiences.

This "replaying" seems to take place during REM sleep (REM, or rapid eye movement, is one of the four sleep stages in which the sleeper's eyes move rapidly back and forth beneath the eyelids). It may be responsible for dreaming, as dreams may be the kaleidoscopic combinations of old and new memories that are being replayed and combined. When dreaming, a person experiences a mixture of what took place during the day and all the associations the mind has made in the past. In this way, long-term memories are formed, and the experiences are compared with what is already known.

Memory consolidation and synapses

In order to understand how memory consolidation functions, it is helpful to understand how neurons work in the brain. Think of it like an electrical system conducting a current- the neurons pass the signals across a synapse from neuron to neuron, with the help of neurotransmitters.

The more frequently signals are passed, the stronger and more plentiful the synaptic connections become, a process, called *potentiation*. Potentiation is believed to play a major role in the learning and memory processes.

When two neurons fire at the same time repeatedly, they become more likely to fire together in the future. Eventually, these two neurons will become sensitized to one another, and as you acquire new experiences, information, and memories, your brain creates more and more of these connections. Essentially, the brain can rearrange itself, establishing new connections while weeding out old ones.

Rehearsing or recalling information repeatedly strengthens these neural networks. For example, if you study the same material regularly over a long period, the pathways involved in remembering that information becomes stronger. The repeated firing of the same neurons makes it more likely that those same neurons will be able to repeat that firing again in the future. As a result, you will be able to remember the information later with greater ease and accuracy. Another way to think of these synaptic pathways is that they are similar to a path in the woods. The more often you walk the path, the more familiar it becomes and the easier it is to travel.

Influences on the memory consolidation process

Through the consolidation process, the brain creates a sort of neural map, allowing memories to be retrieved when they are needed. Experts suggest that sleep can play an important role in the consolidation process. One of the major theories of sleep suggests that sleep exists as a way to process and consolidate information that we have acquired during our waking lives.

People often think of memories as permanent, but just because a memory has been consolidated does not mean that it can't be lost. The process of recalling and reconsolidating a memory can help maintain and strengthen information in long-term memory.

Researchers have also found that memories need to be reconsolidated every time they are accessed. This process, however, can transform and change the memory itself. The very act of remembering, it seems, can actually lead to some things being forgotten.

It is also possible to speed up the consolidation process when learning new information with rehearsal and memorization strategies, such as studying and mnemonic devices. However, one of the best ways to ensure that information is consolidated into long-term memory is to rehearse it over several spaced intervals repeatedly. That's why going over your class notes once a week for several weeks will lead to greater memory retention than cramming the night before an exam.

Memory distribution

Memory distribution is the concept that long-term memories are stored in the relevant sensory cortices: the visual portion of the memory is stored in the visual cortex; the auditory part of the memory is stored in the auditory cortex, and so on.

Two important areas to consider when thinking about memory distribution are how negative experiences are stored and how we would like positive experiences to be stored. Negative experiences are stored and accessed according to what we see, hear, feel, taste, and smell at the time we had the experience. This can lead to a situation in which a person has a strong negative reaction to an environmental stimulus (something the person sees, hears, or smells) that appears totally out of proportion to the stimulus itself.

We see this happening with phobias in which someone has a very strong negative reaction to something that appears to be quite neutral to other people. The reason for the reaction may be that the stimulus for the trigger was present when a strongly negative experience (related to something else entirely) occurred. The stimulus became encoded in memory and serves as an access point to the past experience.

For example, suppose someone experiences intense anxiety when an orange cat is seen. It could be that the person had an intense negative experience in the past when an orange cat was present. This experience was encoded in its entirety, and even though the orange cat has nothing to do with what happened, it still acts as a gateway to the negative experience. Now, whenever the person sees an orange cat, anxiety is felt. This may happen even though the person may not consciously remember the rest of the memory.

Episodic memory

Episodic memory is the memory of past events. If you say, "Every time I have to speak in public, I become afraid," you are talking about a set of past experiences in which the problem happened. It also implies that you expect the problem events to repeat themselves in the future. Most anxiety issues work like this. The anxious person is generating a "future memory", a memory of something that has not yet taken place.

Your subconscious mind is constantly pulling from all of your past experiences to know how to act and react in the moment. For instance, if a dog bit you when you were younger, the fear and trauma of that event leaves a red flag in your memory. Our subconscious is a survival machine, and when an experience carries a strong negative emotional charge, the subconscious says, "Remember this." So, the next time you encounter a dog, the fear kicks in because your mind wants you to be on high alert and either freeze, fight, or run.

Your subconscious triggers fear based on the red flag the bite left in your memory. When you see another dog that growls, you get another dose of the stress chemicals that reinforce the message that dogs are a threat. Then the next time you see a dog, your subconscious knows that fear is the proper response. You don't have to think about it; it is automatic. Your subconscious thinks that is the proper response because it is what you have been doing, and you are still alive, so it is a good strategy for survival.

That is how the mind works. It uses all the past examples of "dog equals danger" to create an unconscious, immediate reaction in the present. This stress response is responsible for keeping our species alive.

If a person who fears dogs changes some of these memories and experiences so that she remembers feeling comfortable and even confident with a dog in one memory and then affection in another, resourceful memories are added to the storehouse of memories that the subconscious mind has to draw from.

Research shows that whether people are remembering or imagining an event – even a fantasy about the future – the exact same parts of the brain light up. On a neurological level, it doesn't matter to the brain if it is accessing a real memory or one that is made up. In fact, the brain doesn't make the distinction between something that is strongly imagined and something that is actually taking place. This means that each time you imagined a dog and were afraid, you reinforced the fear. However, by rehearsing being comfortable and confident in the presence of a dog, your subconscious mind is given new options so you will likely have a neutral or even a positive response the next time you encounter a dog.

Memory reconsolidation

Memories are essentially stored as connections between neurons in the brain. These connections link together various experiences, stimuli, and emotions – which is why hearing a song or smelling cookies can suddenly bring fragments of memories hurtling back. It is unusual for us to forget memories completely, but if they aren't accessed often enough or if they aren't linked to enough cues, there won't be enough strong "in-roads" for us to find them.

This all takes place as a result of the brain's inherent plasticity. The brain, like a muscle, changes shape and size in response to the way we use it. Every experience you have has the effect of altering the layout of your brain, and each time you repeat a movement or experience, you strengthen the pathways that represent it. Sing a song over and over again and the synaptic connections between neurons that encode that song will strengthen. (Specifically, this occurs through the myelination of axons – the thickening of a sheath that protects cells and enhances their conductivity).

Your memory changes every time you access it

The unreliability of memory is something that is well documented and publicized. Like it or not, you can't trust the contents of your memory. The most fascinating reason why is that we constantly alter our memories every time we access them. We don't do this on purpose, but it is an involuntary side effect of the process of activating memories.

Memory reconsolidation is just a fancy name for the idea that each and every time a person remembers something, the memory changes based on what is happening right then at the time the person does the remembering, rather than at the time the event took place.

It is as if the act of remembering lifts the memory out of the brain to be reprocessed and then puts it back in with the new information added. This is startling to most people. We like to think that we remember things the way they happened, and that we can trust our recall, but every time we remember something, we change the memory. Memory reconsolidation is an active and very complex internal process that pulls from many areas of the brain.

Every time you access one of your memories, the same thing happens. The process of retrieving those memories strengthens the connections that lead to it and those that create the complete picture. Meanwhile though, you also create new connections with whatever is going on at the time. Say, for example, you recall an event while at an ice rink. It is likely that you may end up creating a connection that leads you to remember the event as being cold – rightly or wrongly.

At the same time, you form a memory of yourself *remembering* that memory. It is *this* memory that you then retrieve the next time you try and think back – including all the inaccuracies and mistakes from that fabrication. In short, the simple act of remembering something is enough to distort our memory of that event – eventually to the point of it becoming entirely false.

Understanding memory reconsolidation is one of the most important facets to understanding how to work to create change.

If you ask an eyewitness to a car accident, "How fast was the red car driving?" the witness will say something like, "It was going fast, probably at least 100 kilometres per hour!" even if there was no red car there. As soon as you ask the question about the red car, the witness' memory about the car accident is re-consolidated, and the witness remembers the red car being there.

There is a lot of research on this. For example, in one study by Loftus and Palmer, participants were asked to look at a video of an accident, and afterwards, they were asked to estimate how fast the cars in the video were going when they hit each other. The questions were asked in a number of different ways – such as with the word "hit' being replaced with words such as "smashed" or "bumped". When the witnesses were asked how fast the cars were going when they "smashed into each other", they gave a much higher estimate of speed than those witnesses who were asked how fast the cars were going when they "bumped" into each other. How the question was asked influenced the information that went back into the memory of the study participants. This is why lawyers are not allowed to ask leading questions in court and why they still do.

Bear in mind that all Loftus and Palmer did was to ask questions with one word ("smashed") replaced by another word ("bumped"). They weren't even asking the participants to vividly imagine something, nor were they seeking to elicit emotional states. Even so, this simple play on words was sufficient to prime the participants' conscious and subconscious responses.

In another study that took place in the week of the *Challenger* space shuttle disaster, participants were asked about where they were and what was happening around them when they heard about the incident and how they heard about it. Those same study participants were then asked the same questions nine months later and were also asked about how confident they were about the accuracy of their memory. Of course, they were all very confident because they thought, "How could I forget!" Yet a quarter of the subjects gave very inconsistent answers.

We used to think that "flashbulb memory", which is a memory with a very strong emotional reaction, was very accurate because it was burned into consciousness so strongly, but now we are finding that this is not the case at all. The emotionality of flashbulb memory is burned in, but the details fade and change with new information because of reconsolidation. Interestingly, the professor who ran the *Challenger* experiment did so because of a peculiar memory reconsolidation episode that happened to him. He was relating an event that happened to him when his assistant said, "No, that was me! That happened to me; you weren't even in town!" and the professor said, "That's impossible! I clearly remember..." He couldn't believe how absolutely certain he was of a memory that wasn't even his.

Through re-consolidation, we re-remember a memory each time we think about it, and each change we make in a recollection is then re-stored in memory. Our memory can evolve over time. The more times we recall it, the more opportunities it has to change.

But sometimes the changes we make in our memories can be significant. For example, we may have had a conversation with a friend, which we remember as being a pleasant experience. Later on, we discover that our friend has been spreading rumours about us behind our backs, and now, suddenly, all memory of the conversation changes and becomes more negative.

The more you think about your anxiety and times in the past that you have experienced it, the stronger and more reinforced the memories become. Even though the memory may have drastically changed over time.

Although we will swear that they are true, we trust our most updated memory and the original version is lost.

Memory distortion

Memories aren't exact records of events. Instead, memories are reconstructed in many different ways after events happen, which means they can be distorted by several factors. These factors include schemas, source amnesia, the misinformation effect, hindsight bias, the overconfidence effect, and confabulation.

Schemas

A *schema* is a mental representation of an object or event that includes knowledge as well as beliefs and expectations. These are the blueprints we hold in our brain for various things – our prototypical examples of things we see in the world. For instance, we have schemas for what people look like when we picture a scene. Similarly, we have schemas for what lamps look like and what tablecloths look like. We can't pay attention to everything going on around us, so when we remember an environment, we often find ourselves unconsciously "filling in the gaps", based on schemas. Schemas can distort memory.

Example: Suppose a high-school student visits her sister's university dorm room for the first time. She has never been to a dorm before, but she has seen dorms in movies, read about them, and heard her friends talking about them. When she describes the room to another friend after the visit, she comments on how many clothes her sister had and how many huge books were on her sister's desk. In reality, the books were hidden under the bed, not out in the open. The clothes were something she actually saw, while the books were part of her dorm-room schema.

Source amnesia

Another reason for distorted memories is that people often don't accurately remember the origin of information. This inaccurate recall of the origin of information is called source amnesia, source misattribution, or source monitoring error.

Example: After witnessing a car crash on the freeway, Sam later tells friends many details about what he saw. It turns out, however, that there is no way he could have actually seen some of the details he described and that he is, in fact, just reporting details he heard on TV about the accident. He isn't deliberately lying. He just may not be able to remember where all the different pieces of information came from.

The misinformation effect

The misinformation effect occurs when people's recollections of events are distorted by information given to them after the event occurred. Psychologist Elizabeth Loftus did influential research on the misinformation effect that showed that memory reconstructions can affect eyewitness testimony.

Example: A bank robber enters a crowded bank in the middle of the day, waving a gun. He shoots out the security cameras and terrifies everyone. He is taking money from a teller when one of two security guards approaches the robber, draws his own weapon, and shoots. Suddenly, another shot is fired from a different direction, and the first security guard falls to the ground; he has been shot. Some of the customers see that the second security guard, who was approaching the robber from the other side, mistakenly shot his partner. Later, police ask the witnesses when the robber shot the guard, and they report that he shot after the first security guard fired on him. Even though they saw the second security guard shoot the first, they were swayed by the misinformation given by the police.

In one of Loftus' early experiments, she showed research subjects a film of a simulated automobile accident at an intersection with a stop sign. Afterward, she told half the subjects that there was a yield sign at the intersection. When asked later to describe the accident, those who had received the misleading suggestion tended to claim with certainty that there was a yield sign at the intersection, while those subjects who received no misleading suggestions had a more accurate recollection.

Hindsight bias

Hindsight bias is the tendency to interpret the past in a way that fits the present.

Example: If Stella's boyfriend cheats on her, she may recall the boyfriend as always having seemed promiscuous, even if this is not true.

The overconfidence effect

The overconfidence effect is the tendency people have to overestimate their ability to recall events correctly.

Example: A person who thinks he has a photographic memory and a detailed understanding of a subject. The person could show his overconfidence by deciding not to study for a test he has to take on that subject, and doing poorly on the test due to lack of preparation.

Confabulation

Confabulation is a type of memory error in which gaps in a person's memory are unconsciously filled with fabricated, misinterpreted, or distorted information. When a person confabulates, they are confusing things they have imagined with real memories.

A person who is confabulating is not lying. They are not making a conscious or intentional attempt to deceive. Rather, they are confident in the truth of their memories even when confronted with contradictory evidence.

Example: A person may not be able to remember exactly how they got a small bruise on their arm, but may fabricate or misremember a story to explain how the injury occurred.

So, you see, we cannot rely on our memories to be true or accurate. As you now know, memories are unreliable. Every time we recall a memory it is distorted.

Our brains tend to generalize and link situations together. Anxiety can be linked to memories of the past, but because your memories become distorted, your anxiety may not be caused by what you think.

CHAPTER 7

Is your brain playing tricks on you?

We have established that you can't rely on your memories to be an accurate and true recollection of events. So, can you rely on your senses and your thoughts to battle anxiety?

Your brain does regularly "play tricks" on you. It has been scientifically proven that your brain goes about its regular business of automatically processing the sensory inputs of your environment without you ever consciously thinking about it. And as it does this, your brain can fool you into seeing things that aren't there or into not seeing things that are there.

Optical illusions

Optical illusions can use colour, light, and patterns to create images that can be deceptive or misleading to our brains. The information gathered by the eye is processed by the brain to create a perception that does not match the true image.

Here are a few that you may be familiar with:

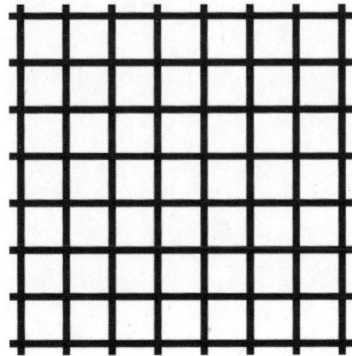

Those grey dots you are seeing in the grid aren't actually there. This is known as a Hermann grid. The dots are the result of a neural process called lateral inhibition – the capacity of an excited neuron to reduce the activity of its neighbours. When a lot of light is let in to a retinal neuron (like the white bands), the neurons can't process all of it, so grey dots appear.

Can you tell how many legs this elephant has? If looking at the legs is giving you a headache, you're not alone. An easy to way solve this problem is to cover the feet. Then you will be able to clearly see that the elephant only has four legs. The reason it looks so trippy is that the artist left the natural space for the feet blank, instead of drawing the feet in the spaces between the legs. This confuses your brain and makes you see the spaces as legs as well.

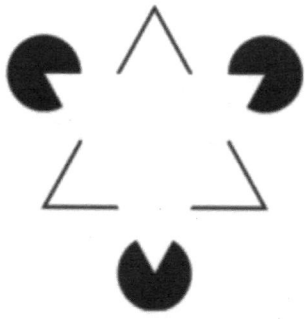

This illusion is called the Kanizsa triangle. Calling this illusion a "triangle" is actually a bit of a misnomer. There are no actual triangles anywhere in the illustration. Your brain fills in the gaps in the line segments and the black circles and assumes there should be a triangle there —also known as the phantom edge phenomenon.

As you saw in the above examples, our eyes send signals to our brains that our brains somehow misinterpret for us, leaving us with false impressions that can be hard to detect even with scrutiny.

Is your mind playing tricks on you?

If we can't believe our eyes or our memories, can we rely on our thoughts? Unfortunately, not always, as sometimes we experience cognitive distortions.

Cognitive Distortions

Cognitive distortions are ways that our mind convinces us of something that isn't really true. These inaccurate thoughts are usually used to reinforce negative thinking or emotions telling ourselves things that sound rational and accurate, but really only serve to keep us feeling badly about ourselves.

We often don't realize that we are doing this. Unfortunately, our thoughts can become so automatic that we begin to take them as reality, even if that is not actually the case.

By learning to correctly identify this kind of negative, sabotaging thinking, a person can then understand it is wrong and reject it. Becoming aware of our cognitive distortions enables us to shift our thought patterns and thus improve the quality of our lives.

Reframing (also referred to as "cognitive reframing") is a technique used to help create a different way of looking at a situation, person, or relationship by changing its meaning. Reframing is a strategy that therapists often use to help clients look at situations from a slightly different perspective.

The essential idea behind reframing is that a person's point of view depends on the frame it is viewed in. When the frame is shifted, the meaning changes and thinking and behaviour often change along with it.

Reframing 13 common cognitive distortions

1. IF I'M NOT FIRST, I'M LAST.
Cognitive distortion: All or nothing thinking
The belief that "if you don't win, you lose" is a form of all-or-nothing thinking. Also referred to as black-and-white thinking, this type of cognitive distortion sees everything as black or white and fails to miss the many shades of grey in between. Another common phrase that exemplifies this type of dichotomous thinking is: "If it weren't for bad luck, I'd have no luck at all." The reality is that everyone has misfortunes every now and then. You win some. You lose some.

To see things as only one way or the other can seriously limit your thinking and lead to negative emotions.

Reframe: I didn't place first, but third place is pretty good. I'm proud of myself, and I'll try even harder next time.

2. IF I HAD JUST BEEN THERE FOR HIM/HER, THIS WOULDN'T HAVE HAPPENED.
Cognitive distortion: personalization

When we tell ourselves things like this, we are taking personal responsibility for events that are actually out of our control. This type of distorted thinking is referred to as personalization. A person engaged in personalisation takes everything personally and sees themself at the centre of every situation.

The reality is that sometimes unfortunate things happen to people that we love and nothing we personally did or didn't do could have changed that.

Reframe: I accept that some things are out of my control, and there is nothing in my personal power that I can do to change them.

3. I ALWAYS MESS THINGS UP. I'LL NEVER GET ANYWHERE IN LIFE.
Cognitive distortion: Overgeneralization
Anytime you use the words "always", "never", "ever", "every", or "all", it is likely that you are overgeneralizing. If you make one mistake, and you instantly tell yourself, "I always mess things up", "I never do anything right", or "I'll never get better", it is time to take a good look at your thinking patterns. The reality is that you cannot draw conclusions from one, two, or even three single events. Just because you have made a mistake or two, doesn't mean you are a failure.

Reframe: I've made a few mistakes, but I am learning. There is always room for improvement.

4. ANYTHING THAT CAN GO WRONG WILL GO WRONG.
Cognitive distortion: Fortune telling
This form of cognitive distortion referred to as fortune telling involves using this phrase to arbitrarily predict negative outcomes in the future. **In reality, there are many possibilities for the future. Some outcomes are positive, and some negative.** Wouldn't you rather be hopeful and optimistic about the future than look at it from a "doom and gloom" perspective?

Reframe: Every cloud has a silver lining. Even if something undesirable happens, there is still something to be gained from the situation.

5. I'M NOT GOOD ENOUGH.
Cognitive distortion: Labelling
This is something we have all probably told ourselves a time or two in our lives. Telling ourselves that we aren't good enough can shatter our confidence and keep us from taking risks or trying new things in life. Labelling is a more severe type of over-generalization in which people label themselves negatively. **The reality is that whether it is "I'm not good enough", "I'm a failure", or "I'm such a loser", none of these statements are true, nor will they make you feel good about yourself.** Try replacing these thoughts with positive affirmations and work to achieve a balance where you also recognize your strengths. Remind yourself of situations when you have been successful in your goals.

Reframe: I am good enough. I can be self-compassionate and accept myself just the way I am.

6. I SHOULD HAVE ___ AND THEN ____.
Cognitive distortion: Should statements
An example of this type of thinking is: "I should have worn the black tie to the interview and maybe I would have gotten the job." If you find yourself using the words "should have", "would have", "could have", "ought to have", or "must", then you are likely engaging in a cognitive distortion. Try reframing the situation to see what you can learn from it rather than focusing on what you "should" have done differently. **The reality is that should statements serve no purpose other than to create negative emotions like guilt, shame, anger, or regret. We cannot change the past.** Telling yourself that you should have done this or you could have done that doesn't change the fact that you didn't do the thing in question.

Reframe: I didn't do ____, but I can't change the past. However, I can learn from this experience and do things differently in the future.

7. I FEEL LIKE HE/SHE LIED TO ME, SO HE/SHE MUST HAVE.

Cognitive distortion: Emotional reasoning

Just because you feel a certain way doesn't mean that it is accurate. For example, a person can feel scared even if there is no real external threat. A person engaged in emotional reasoning often mistakes their feelings for reality. It is best to look at situations objectively and detach from your emotions before making any critical judgments. **The reality is that we all have intuition from time to time. Sometimes we have a gut feeling, and it turns out to be right, but our feelings do not equal reality.**

Reframe: I have a feeling that he lied to me, but that doesn't necessarily mean he did. I will tell him how I feel and give him a chance to tell his side of the story.

8. WHEN IT RAINS, IT POURS.

Cognitive distortion: Catastrophizing

We've all heard the adage, "When it rains, it pours". It often seems like when one thing goes wrong, everything starts to go wrong. But some people engaged in negative thinking take this to the extreme. Catastrophizing is a cognitive distortion where people make a mountain out of a molehill. They blow small things out of proportion and turn them into big things. This is a person who fails one exam and assumes he will fail the entire course. The reality is that a little sprinkle is not the same thing as a downpour.

Reframe: Yes, there was a little bit of rain during our camping trip, but at least it wasn't a thunderstorm.

9. IT'S ALL HER/HIS FAULT.

Cognitive distortion: Blaming

This cognitive distortion is the opposite of personalization. Instead of seeing something as "all my fault", a person engaged in blaming becomes a victim who always sees the fault as belonging to someone else. **The reality is that, regardless of the situation you are in, it is**

never all someone else's fault. You will always have some degree of responsibility for the events that take place in your life. Rather than point the finger at someone else, take the time to reflect on the part you played and take full personal responsibility for your own actions.

Reframe: I take responsibility for my role in the situation.

10. I CAN TELL PEOPLE DON'T LIKE ME.
Cognitive distortion: Mind reading
A person engaged in mind reading assumes that he is psychic and can read the mind of others even if there is no outward confirmation of it being true. If you find yourself saying things like, "I can tell people don't like me," stop and examine the situation. Do you really have any evidence that this is true? The reality is that we can't know what someone else is thinking unless we ask them, and if we think we do, we are making assumptions based on our own insecurities.

Reframe: I cannot read other people's minds. It is possible that I am projecting my own insecurities on to others.

11. I'M NOBODY SPECIAL. ANYBODY COULD DO WHAT I DO.
Cognitive distortion: Minimizing
A person engaged in this cognitive distortion can never do anything right as he will always minimize his own accomplishments. Unfortunately, the same person who minimizes the good in his life will usually maximize and overgeneralize the bad. The reality is that it is okay to give yourself a pat on the back for your achievements. You deserve it. If you find yourself downplaying your own strengths and talents, try shifting your thinking and praising yourself instead.

Reframe: I have worked really hard to achieve what I have. It is okay to be proud of myself.

12. IF THEY HAVEN'T CALLED BY NOW, THE NEWS MUST BE BAD.

Cognitive distortion: Jumping to conclusions

Jumping to conclusions and assuming the worst just because time has passed will only create anxiety and other negative emotions within you. In these situations, it is best to be both patient and realistic. The reality is that jumping to conclusions before you have all the evidence is unlikely to result in an accurate conclusion anyway, so you are just wasting your time and energy.

Reframe: The doctor hasn't called yet, but the office may be busy. I'll wait until I hear something before I make assumptions.

13. HE/SHE COMPLIMENTED ME, BUT HE/SHE WAS JUST BEING NICE.

Cognitive distortion: Discounting the positive

It is all too common for people to discount compliments. Someone says, "I like your shirt," and you respond, "This old thing?" Brushing off compliments tends to be just a start for those who discount the positive. People who engage in this negative thinking pattern tend to discount anything and everything positive in their lives.

The reality is that nothing is all negative or all positive, but by always ignoring the positive, you can suck the enjoyment out of your life and be left feeling inadequate, anxiety ridden, or just plain miserable. Rather than discount the positive, make it count. Soak it in and enjoy it. You'll be glad you did.

Reframe: It feels really good to be complimented. I am grateful for his kind words. And there is at least a 50% possibility he is right.

If, as you read the above list of cognitive distortions, you began to feel the disconcerting feeling that many of them applied to you, that is not necessarily a bad thing. It is not a good thing to be mired in negative and false thoughts, but it *is good* that you are becoming *aware* of the fact that you do so. Now you can begin the work of correcting these destructive thought patterns and consequently begin to feel better.

If you recognize any of these thought patterns within yourself, don't fret: You can retrain your brain.

CHAPTER 8

Neuroplasticity – your brain's superpower

As discussed earlier, neuroplasticity is the brain's ability to reorganize itself by forming new neural connections throughout life. It is the brain's ability to adapt.

Our brains are truly amazing; unlike computers, which are built to certain specifications and receive software updates periodically, our brains can actually receive hardware updates in addition to software updates. Different pathways form and fall dormant, according to our experiences.

When we learn something new, we create new connections between our neurons. We rewire our brains to adapt to new circumstances. This happens on a daily basis, but it is also something we can encourage and stimulate.

Why is neuroplasticity important? Before the discovery of neuroplasticity, it was thought that the only way a person could change their brain was through outside influences such as brain surgery or psychoactive pharmaceutical drugs. Experience dependent neuroplasticity has proven that you can change your brain simply by using your mind in different way.

Neuroscientist Helen Mayberg demonstrated that patients with depression showed the same changes in brain function using placebos as patients who received antidepressant drugs. So if it wasn't the antidepressant drugs creating changes in the brain, what was it? As it turns out, it was the mind. A more specific answer comes from other researchers, including, Dr. Jeffrey Schwartz, who devised a simple protocol to assist patients with Obsessive-Compulsive Disorder (OCD) to change their minds, and from that, change their brains.

In Schwartz's study, participants were divided into two groups: one group took psychoactive drugs (the control group) and the test group was taught a simple four-step mental protocol. The brains of both groups were scanned prior to the treatments and then again after 10–12 weeks. The research team found that the same positive brain structure changes occurred in both the control group who took the drugs and the test group who followed the four-step protocol. By simply thinking about their OCD in a different way, the test group physically changed the structure of their brains and did so without any nasty side effects of medication.

Swartz proved that thinking about problems in a different way leads the patient beyond what the medical establishment considers "placebo", in that it made a real observable change in the physical structure of the brain. It created the same physical change as medication. Further, when a patient stops taking the drugs, the brain may revert to the old loop, while the patients receiving change work therapy learned a skill that makes change self-directed. The patient can continue to make positive changes in her life simply by using her own mind.

The placebo affect is obviously a good thing, but the pharmaceutical companies don't think so. They must test all new drugs against a placebo, and no matter how good the results are, if the drug doesn't beat the placebo, pharma companies can't sell it. Unfortunately for them, they can't sell the placebo either. Through Dr. Schwartz's research, we can see that changing the way we think about a problem has the same physical impact on the brain as drugs, and therefore, is more than simply a placebo.

Your Toolkit contains techniques that are fast, empowering, and rewarding and give you a variety of ways to rewire your brain. You will learn how to stop the anxiety immediately and access the parasympathetic nervous system, which controls homeostasis and the body at rest, as opposed to the sympathetic nervous system which controls the body's response to a perceived threat and is responsible for the "fight-or-flight" response.

Self-directed neuroplasticity

Self-directed neuroplasticity is a just a fancy way of saying that you are using your own mind to change the physical structure of your own brain.

If you read emotional words, your brain activity flows towards the emotional centres as well as the areas that process language. If you read an action word – a compelling story about running, like a chase scene – at some point, your mind is going to start the "running" program in your brain. This means that we don't have to physically do an activity to stimulate the neural networks involved. This allows us to rewire the circuits through imagination and rehearsal. When the brains of athletes who are visualizing sports practice are scanned, the same areas in the brain used when the sport is physically practised light up. The visualization training allows the athletes to outperform, in a very significant way, those athletes who only do physical training.

Experience-dependent neuroplasticity

Current research proves the mind can indeed alter the physical structure of the brain with every new experience a person has. This is called experience-dependent neuroplasticity.

If you are having trouble making changes in your life, it may be because of your neural pathways. For example, if one day you eat because of a craving, a reaction, or a compulsion (and not because you were really and truly "hungry"), the chances are now greater that you will do so again. With each successive time, the chances of repeating the behaviour become more likely. This is because you are reinforcing the neural network and going down the same old road or pathway. The easiest and most effective way to break habituated patterns in the brain is by interrupting them.

Each time you interrupt the pattern, even after just three or four times, other areas of the brain start to be engaged and make new connections. Neurons are making friends with other neurons. Each detour means that the old path gets less use and, therefore, weakens or gets overgrown while the new path gets created. Think of it like a forest. First you have to cut through it to make a clearing for a path. Now each time you walk down the new path, you widen and deepen it so that walking along it gets easier. Each time you start to feel anxiety and immediately use one of the techniques you learn in this book, you will detour into the parasympathetic response. In travelling the new path, the old path becomes idle and starts to disappear as the old neural connections are pruned away.

You are not just stopping the feeling of anxiety; you are rewiring the pattern.

Neural pathways

The basic idea of change is to attach a new neural pathway onto the trigger that used to lead us to the problem. Once this new pathway is successfully installed, the section of the pathway representing the problem will begin to be pruned; it will become divorced from the context in which it used to occur. If it is not needed elsewhere, its neurons will ultimately begin to be used for other purposes. Of course, depending on the intensity of the problem and the amount of time you have been carrying it, the old pathway may be very well developed and, as a result, it may take more time to be pruned entirely.

Once you understand that you are generating the anxiety and that it didn't just come from out of nowhere, you can begin to change it.

The brain is flexible and capable of changing even the most ingrained patterns. Luckily the brain can be rewired more easily than most people imagine.

By using the techniques in your Toolkit, you will interrupt your old anxiety pattern. You are widening out that new pathway, and it will get easier and easier for your mind to choose the new path as the old one begins to grow over.

CHAPTER 9

Effective therapies for anxiety

Many people focus on where they are instead of where they want to be. That's like programming your current location into your GPS and expecting it to go somewhere. It doesn't work.

Albert Einstein said it best when he came up with his famous definition of insanity – doing things the same way over and over, and hoping for or expecting different results. If you have been consistently trying to stop worry and negative thought processes, you would think by now that you would see some results. Have you? I'm guessing you haven't.

If you want to eliminate your anxiety, it is important to do it in the most effective way.

Cognitive Behaviour Therapy

Cognitive Behaviour Therapy (CBT) is one of the most highly recommended and well-respected therapies of the 21st century for the treatment of anxiety.

The basic premise of Cognitive Behaviour Therapy is that our thoughts influence our feelings, which then influence our actions.

Thinking is a habit. It can be a good habit or a bad habit depending on the outcome. Your feelings and behaviours are also habitual when you think the same way, even if that way of thinking is destructive or anxiety provoking.

When you engage in a certain way of thinking, feeling, and acting for a period of time, for example worrying, you will most likely become worried – you're the end result of your thinking, feeling and acting. CBT helps you become aware of inaccurate or negative thinking so you can view challenging situations more clearly and respond to them in a more effective way. An unhealthy thought or being stuck in an unhealthy thought pattern can lead to actions that make the problem worse or keep us trapped in the same situation, basically spinning our wheels and experiencing anxiety over and over again. CBT focuses on the here and now.

CBT gives you a new way of understanding and thinking about your problem. It also provides you with the skills to deal with the issues you are struggling with right now.

CBT enables a person to think more realistically, which leads to feeling better emotionally and behaving more functionally. Distorted thinking has a negative effect on a person's behaviour.

The greatest strength of CBT is that you are taught to live in the present – instead of worrying about "what ifs" in the future. This can have an immediate impact on a person's mindset.

Research shows that CBT is one of the most effective treatments for anxiety. In a systematic review of 27 studies published in the Journal of Clinical Psychiatry (2008), psychologists Hoffman and Smits found that CBT has proven to be an unquestionably successful treatment for adult anxiety disorders. However, they concluded that there was considerable room for improvement.

Anxiety disorders sometimes require the use of two or more treatment methods that are flexible and adjustable to one another. According to Kirsch, Lynn, Rhue, and Schoenberger (American Psychological Association, 1996), hypnosis is an effective treatment for anxiety and can be easily combined with current cognitive and behaviour interventions.

Hypnotherapy

Hypnotherapy uses guided relaxation, intense concentration, and focused attention to achieve the highly relaxed mental state of hypnosis. In this deeply relaxed state, the mind is ready to learn. The person's attention is so focused while in this state that anything going on around the person is temporarily blocked out or ignored. Thus, a person may focus his or her attention – with the help of a trained therapist – on specific thoughts or tasks, such as dealing with anxiety.

While hypnosis has been in use by different names for hundreds of years, in the past it was shrouded in mystery and widely believed to be just trickery – like magic – by those who practiced it. It wasn't until the last century, as we began to explore the frontiers of the brain and advance our understanding of cognitive science, that researchers realized hypnosis is grounded in the working principles of the mind.

It is no longer a question of: Does hypnosis work to help people with medical, emotional, and habit challenges? Rather, today research is focused on understanding "how it works". Hypnosis has proven to be a very effective method of dealing with anxiety, and in fact, hypnosis is now a common complementary medical service in a number of world-renowned healthcare facilities. For example, the Mayo Clinic offers hypnosis as a therapy for pain management, addiction, and anxiety.

Contrary to common misconceptions, hypnosis is actually a natural phenomenon. In fact, people experience shallow hypnotic states several times a day. Examples of this include daydreaming, being so absorbed by a book or movie that you do not hear someone calling your name, or when you have been driving and do not remember how you got to your destination.

However, most of the time, we are distracted by our surroundings – whether it is the TV blaring, kids demanding attention, or your spouse talking to you. In addition, our conscious minds are cluttered. We may be worried about paying a bill, concerned about an upcoming project, or planning tonight's dinner. Day-to-day concerns tend to distract us from focusing on our daily reality. But what is reality?

Reality is formed by our preconceived beliefs. Hypnosis provides a means of overriding these existing beliefs, assumptions, and memories. Here's an example of the power of our preconditioned beliefs. A group of participants were asked to take a wine taste test. They were given two choices: a glass of "expensive" wine and another of moderately priced wine. The participants expected the "expensive wine" to taste better and, therefore, they gave it much higher marks for taste. The suggestion was subtle – one was more expensive – but it shows how easily a suggestion is used to construct our perception. By the way – the two glasses of wine were from the same bottle.

Your subconscious mind may have preconceived beliefs about your anxiety. For example, you might automatically think that eliminating anxiety is impossible because other methods of dealing with anxiety haven't worked. These kinds of subconscious thoughts – which are shaped by memories, experiences, and expectations – ultimately drive our conscious actions, and we don't even realize this is happening.

However, while in the relaxed state of hypnosis, we're able to reframe our thinking patterns because of two principles: disassociation and suggestion.

During hypnosis, because we are able to disassociate our behavioural controls and critical thoughts, the mind is free to act on a suggestion without questioning why or how. The mind can focus and respond differently to create a new reality in which healthier, more helpful responses are triggered by sensory data. For example, if you experience anxiety, your mind may encourage you to react with a fight-or-flight response, but through suggestion, hypnotherapy allows you to update and reframe these responses to be calm and rational. Hypnotherapy empowers us to believe suggestions that best serve us and enables us to alter negative behaviour and reactions.

Hypnosis and neural pathways

One of the most interesting aspects of using hypnosis is how it can change neural pathways. The longer you do something repeatedly, the more likely you are going to do it out of habit. The reason habit forms is because neural pathways in the brain become conditioned to act and respond in a certain way. By changing the neural pathways, you change the way you think. Hypnosis can be used to interrupt damaging patterns when they occur. Pattern-interrupts can eliminate anxiety.

Under hypnosis, you would be asked to think of or just imagine a situation that would normally trigger anxiety and see yourself experiencing the situation free of anxiety. This technique is called future pacing. It allows you to go into the future and experience what it would be like to go through the change you want to make, such as not feeling anxiety. In hypnosis, the mind makes this very real to the person experiencing it. Studies have shown that there is no difference between thinking you can do something and doing it. If you think you can, you can. Thinking about the experience has the same effect on the neural pathways as physically having the experience. Your brain is rewired either way. This forges a new neural pathway in the brain.

Combining Cognitive Behaviour Therapy and Hypnosis

The use of Cognitive Behaviour Therapy with Hypnosis is called Cognitive Behavioural Hypnotherapy (CBH).

The addition of hypnosis to CBT helps the client in several aspects of therapy, such as the preparation for real-life experiences, imagery exposure, development of coping skills, and cognitive restructuring. Clients undergoing CBH effectively develop a better sense of self-efficacy (or belief in their own abilities to deal with various situations), which is known to enhance self-regulation. This is linked to lower psychological distress and better quality of life.

By completing a meta-analysis of 18 studies, University of Connecticut researchers Kirsch, Montgomery, and Sapirstein found that the addition of hypnosis to CBT substantially enhanced the treatment outcome for several problems (obesity, pain, etc.), including the treatment of anxiety disorders. For example, "The average client receiving cognitive behaviour hypnotherapy showed greater improvement than at least 70% of the clients receiving non-hypnotic treatment." The basis of this study was that hypnosis could enhance therapy outcome through its effects on the client's beliefs and expectations.

So, we know that cognitive behaviour therapy and hypnotherapy are effective in the treatment of anxiety. Another very effective way to deal with anxiety is mindfulness.

Mindfulness

What does it really mean to be mindful? Basically, being mindful is about being present and noticing reality as it is in each moment as it unfolds.

Mindfulness is paying attention to the present moment without judgment. The idea of staying in the moment is a skill that comes easily with practice. Mindfulness is not meditating for thirty minutes while assuming unusual postures or wearing unconventional clothes. In fact, a person doesn't even need to be still to practice mindfulness.

You can shop mindfully. You can walk mindfully. You can sit mindfully, or you can eat mindfully. The goal in mindfulness is not to empty your mind or to stop thinking, as in meditation. On the contrary, it is simply to give us time to allow ourselves to observe ourselves experiencing our own thoughts.

Research shows that people spend most or all of their day being anything but mindful. They skip from one thought to another. They daydream. They ruminate about their past. They worry about the future. They self-analyze and self-criticize.

Results of research indicate that mindfulness can help you in more ways than you might think. Liddy and Good performed a study of over 4,000 scientific papers on various degrees of mindfulness. They looked at the impact of mindfulness in terms of how people think, feel, and perform at work. It was discovered that mindfulness positively impacts attention and can help one remain focused on the present. Those who completed mindfulness training were better able to remain vigilant and focused, especially on visual and listening tasks. Mindfulness also can help improve cognition, emotions, physiology, and even behaviour.

Most importantly for those who suffer from anxiety, people who are taught and practice mindfulness reduce worrying.

Another interesting study on mindfulness was conducted by Sara Lazar, a neuroscientist at the Harvard Medical School. In this study, Lazar tested participants for the positive effects that mindfulness practice would have on psychological well-being. Lazar was also interested in helping alleviate symptoms of chronic pain, insomnia, depression, and anxiety, amongst other things.

After eight weeks, the participants were examined and the results showed that their hippocampus structure had increased. The study results also showed that their amygdala had decreased, which meant the fight-or-flight response, the reaction to threats, also decreased.

All of this research is promising because it means that the change in people's reactions occurs within themselves and not in the environment. In fact, new research suggests people with anxiety can begin to derive psychological and physiological benefits from the practice of mindfulness after a single introductory session. In addition, researchers said most participants reported continuing to use mindfulness after the initial session and anxiety scores were reduced even further one week later.

Mindfulness practice rebalances neural networks, allowing you to move away from automatic, negative anxiety responses and to understand that there are other ways to respond to situations. Recent studies have also shown that including mindfulness exercises in your daily routine cuts down the production of the stress hormone cortisol and reduces feelings of anxiety and fatigue. Therefore, using mindfulness techniques throughout the day could help you strike a more effective work-life balance.

The Toolkit in this book teaches you mindfulness, and you will practice mindfulness each time you listen to your audio recording. You could read volumes about mindfulness, but the best way to learn it is to experience it. You will be guided through a peaceful, mindfulness practice session every night, while you rest and relax.

We have looked at the benefits of Cognitive Behaviour Therapy, Hypnotherapy, and Mindfulness, and each has their own merits.

However, in order to deal with anxiety, a more comprehensive approach is necessary.

Combining Cognitive Behaviour Therapy and Mindfulness

Many studies have been done on the effects of combining CBT and Mindfulness. One of the most widely recognized therapies includes Mindfulness-Based Cognitive Therapy (MBCT), which was developed by Segal, Williams, and Teasdale. The goal of MBCT is to help people change thoughts that are unproductive. This might include patterns of thought that aren't serving you well or other types of behaviours and emotional responses.

Like Cognitive Behaviour Therapy and hypnotherapy, MCTB focuses on the here and now. Rather than try to avoid or eliminate anxiety, you learn to change your relationship with anxiety by practicing mindfulness.

Cognitive Behaviour Therapy, Mindfulness, and Hypnosis as a treatment method for anxiety

Many clinicians notice improvements in clients through the separate modalities of Cognitive Behaviour Therapy, Hypnotherapy, and Mindfulness, but these individual methods can fall short. Researchers have found that it can be far more effective to combine these three methods into one protocol.

The effectiveness of CBT on anxiety is well supported by empirical research and is often considered the gold standard. However, studies indicate that CBT does not address all of the obstacles or blockages of those who suffer from anxiety and that the exploration and integration of other therapies is necessary to improve overall treatment. As a result, mindfulness and hypnosis methods, both of which contain relaxation elements considered essential to the treatment of anxiety, have emerged as important methods in new anxiety treatment models. Because CBT recipients continue to struggle with post-treatment anxiety, practitioners increasingly turn to other therapy tools for improved and longer lasting outcomes for their patients.

Mindfulness training treats anxiety through adjustments to cognitive processes and patterns. It has proven so effective that it is rapidly gaining in popularity among practitioners. Mindfulness approaches are based on the premise that rather than trying to avoid or suppress an experience, the person should simply allow it to occur.

Paying attention to their breath trains the person to attend to the present moment; it is particularly applicable in treating the anxious person who focuses on the future – specifically, what might go wrong in the future. General anxiety patients have shown significant improvement in reducing their levels of worry, anxiety, and depression after treatment, and the majority of benefits were still apparent at a three-month follow up. Redirecting the mind to the present moment steers patients toward more healthy thinking patterns and processes.

Hypnosis research suggests it is also a highly effective treatment method for anxiety and anxiety-related disorders. Hypnosis has some similarities to mindfulness, such as sitting quietly and focussing attention. However, in hypnosis, the clinician also uses interventions to allow the client to focus on his or her experience and provides an opportunity to engage with new possibilities (e.g. considering changes in sensation, perceptions, thoughts, or behaviours).

Unlike mindfulness or CBT, hypnosis is typically oriented toward a specific goal (e.g. to stop smoking or lose weight) and is less focused on the generalized notion of "letting go" associated with mindfulness. Also, unlike mindfulness or CBT, research has shown that hypnosis may actually serve as a catalyst, magnifying the effects of mindfulness when the methods are combined.

What is exciting about the blending of these different treatments is that research has shown time and again that these types of treatment plans promote positive client outcomes, and it is even more effective to combine these three methods into an integrative protocol.

Making the sum greater than the whole

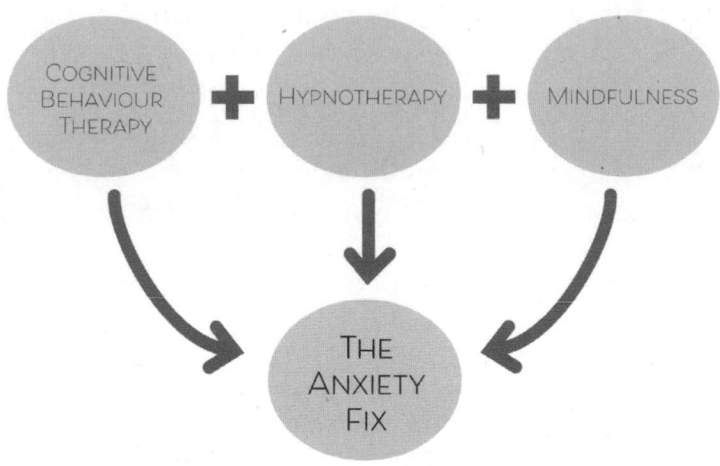

CHAPTER 10

The Anxiety Fix Toolkit

The techniques set out in this section provide simple, easy-to-use-and-remember strategies to interrupt the anxiety pattern and change your neural pathways. You will learn new skills and strategies to change old thinking patterns that may have been years in the making.

At the beginning of this book you were given the information to download the audio recording that is part of *The Anxiety Fix* Toolkit.

It is very important that you do not listen to this recording while driving or operating machinery.

Only listen to this recording when you can rest comfortably, undisturbed for about **30** minutes. You will be guided into relaxation and mindfulness. Ideally you can listen to this recording every night when you go to bed. Simply lay back, relax, and let your subconscious mind do the work.

Pattern-interrupt techniques

The goal of pattern-interrupt is to stop your existing thought patterns before they travel down a neural pathway to anxiety. Use these quick and easy techniques whenever you start to feel anxiety creeping in on you.

Most people have a difficult time creating a pattern-interrupt on their own as their minds are too fixated on their old thought patterns. With that said, most people experience pattern-interrupt on a daily basis whenever they are distracted by unexpected noises, movements, and other people talking or when they engage in activities that relax or calm them, such as working out, going for a long walk, meditating, or even taking a different route home from work.

It's all about shifting your perspective.

Try out each one of the following techniques as you read them. Once you become familiar with them before the anxiety is in full swing, you will be armed and ready when you need to be. Whenever you feel anxiety starting to well up or a panic attack starting, use one of the pattern-interrupt exercises. The techniques will neutralize triggers and reprogram your neural pathways.

Practice your favourites so they become second nature to you. Make these your familiar go-to whenever anxiety pops up. These techniques not only give you immediate relief; you are slowly but surely dismantling the neural network that used to keep that anxiety alive. These techniques will give you many ways to calm, inform, and change the bully in your brain.

Mindfulness

The first step in dealing with anxiety is being present or in other words – mindful. The best way to learn mindfulness is to experience it. I guarantee that when you practice mindfulness daily, you will find the value of it is incredible. It is one of your biggest weapons against anxiety.

Here is a quick mindfulness exercise that you can use anytime. This effective technique will aleviate your anxiety state quickly and easily.

Mentally scan your body and loosen any muscles that are holding tension. Relax your jaw and let your shoulders drop. Let your eyelids and hands become heavy with relaxation as you just breathe. You don't have to try to speed up or slow down your breathing. All you need go do is breathe and pay attention to each breath. There is not a right way or wrong way to do this. It is simply the practice of paying attention.

Observe your breath; notice the tempo of your breath and the temperature of the air. Observe how the air flows in, and what it feels when it flows out. We breathe everyday, all day, usually without noticing it. By practicing an awareness of your breathing, you are really practicing an awareness of this moment.

As you breathe in and out, label the breath. Call it by its name. Label the in breath "in" and call the out breath "out". Say to yourself: "in ... out." Notice the air as you breathe in and the point where the air in your lungs turns around and becomes an exhalation. As you pay attention to each breath, you'll also notice that you are aware of sounds and sensations apart from your breath. The practice is not to stop noticing these things, but rather, when you do notice these, simply note that you are doing that and return your attention to your breath.

If you notice yourself thinking about anything at all, you do not have to try to stop thinking. Just note the thought instead of following it. Simply say to yourself, "That is a thought." Bring your attention back to your breath. If you become aware of an emotion during this time, this is okay. Simply say to yourself, "That is an emotion." The practice here is not to suppress them, but not to follow them. Simply note them and say to yourself, "That is a feeling," and return your attention to your breath.

Likewise, if you have any sensations in your body, you can simply note that is what your body feels without becoming engaged in it or following it. Just use it as a cue to return your attention to your breath, noticing what it feels like to breathe in and out.

Each time your mind begins to follow a thought or a feeling or an awareness of a sensation, gently, without judgment, return your attention to your breath. It doesn't matter how many times you need to do this. The value is in developing the practice of returning to the moment by returning your awareness to your breath.

Breathe in and out for a few minutes, paying attention to your breath. Continue until you feel yourself becoming more grounded and the anxiety is released.

Bilateral stimulation

This simple technique is one of my favourites because it is easy and can be done discretely anywhere. Bilateral stimulation works by stimulating both hemispheres of the brain. It is incredibly simple and amazingly effective. Grab a ball (or pen or anything small that you can toss) and then think of something that is causing you anxiety.

When you experience a situation and feel the onset of anxiety, rate the level of it on a scale of one to ten.

Now pass the ball/object back and forth, from one hand to the other, crossing the mid-line of your body, so you are stimulating both hemispheres of the brain. It will work more quickly if you keep one hand in front of you as the other swings out to the side each time you pass the ball/object. Do this for a minute. Stop. Take a deep breath and check-in. You might note that the anxiety has dissipated.

By activating both hemispheres of your brain, you are increasing blood and electrical impulses throughout the brain, and this floods that area of association and diffuses it. The anxiety cluster just can't keep itself together.

Now, think of the same situation again and see how much anxiety you can manage to conjure up, and rate it once again on the one-to-ten scale. Pass the ball/object for another minute and check-in. Repeat the process until the anxiety has completely diffused.

As soon as you start to feel that anxiety, simply grab any suitable object like keys or a bottle of water – anything will work – as long as you are moving both your arms and crossing the mid-line of your body.

Deep and slow breathing (and your vagus nerve)

The vagus nerve is the longest nerve in your body. It connects your brain to many important organs throughout the body, including the gut (intestines, stomach), heart, and lungs.

The vagus nerve is a key part of your parasympathetic "rest and digest" nervous system. It influences your breathing, digestive function, and heart rate, all of which can have a huge impact on your mental health.

By developing an understanding of the workings of your vagus nerve, you may find it possible to work with your nervous system rather than feeling trapped when it works against you. Stimulating your vagus nerve can play a key role in the management of your mental health.

Deep and slow breathing is one way to stimulate your vagus nerve. It has been shown to reduce anxiety and increase parasympathetic system activity.

Take a moment to relax your jaw as much as you can. Loosen it even more, and imagine it dropping to the floor.

When you drop your jaw, you are stimulating the parasympathetic nervous system to counteract the fight-or-flight response controlled by the sympathetic nervous system. You are also encouraging the lungs to take a deep breath, creating a flood of biochemicals associated with the relaxation response.

Most people take about 10 to 14 breaths each minute. Taking about 6 breaths over the course of a minute is a great way to relieve stress.

Relax your jaw, take a deep breath in, and pause for a count of three. Then exhale twice as long through the nose. When you inhale deeply, put your hand on your belly and feel it rise; this ensures that you are using your diaphragm to draw in your breath (belly breathing). Your exhalation should be long and slow. This is key to stimulating the vagus nerve and reaching a state of relaxation.

Some people find that by inhaling to a count of four, pausing for three, and exhaling for eight, they are able keep their mind from ruminating as they allow the relaxation response to merge with their breathing.

By stimulating the vagus nerve, you can send a message to your body that it is time to relax and de-stress, which leads to long-term improvements in mood, well- being, and anxiety resilience.

Peripheral vision

Try this simple way of shifting out of your mind to neutralize anxious internal dialogue.

Start by picking a focal point to stare at. Slowly begin to expand your peripheral vision to include all the space around the spot. Now expand your vision even further to the sides, all the way up to the ceiling, and down to the floor. Expand it even more, allowing your visual field to open so that you can imagine almost becoming aware of the space behind you.

This might feel strange at first, but after practicing three or four times, you will notice a general calm come over your mind and body as you realize your internal dialogue has stopped.

This is sometimes called "stopping the world". This technique allows you to move awareness from "inside" to "outside" when experiencing anxiety.

The great thing about "peripheral vision" is that it can be done anywhere, anytime.

Changing internal dialogue

The other way to change your neural pathways is to notice and manipulate the internal dialogue you are running that keeps the anxiety going.

As soon as you start feeling anxious, notice what you say to yourself. Guaranteed it is not helpful or supportive. We are very good at feeding our anxiety by talking to ourselves in a negative way. Once you have become aware of this, you can begin to manipulate that "negative" self-talk.

For example, if you replay a phrase your first boyfriend or girlfriend said to you and many years later it is still making you feel worthless, ask yourself now, as an adult, would you ever take the words of a sixteen-year-old to heart? Now let the negative belief you had about yourself evaporate.

Another effective method is to add the word "so" to the beginning of a worry statement to change the impact it has on you. You can change, "What if they don't like me?" to "So what if they don't like me?" and "What if I can't do this?" to "So what if I can't do this?"

Try this out. You might be surprised at how simple this two-letter word can change how you feel.

Using these different ways of manipulating internal dialogue will help to make your worry statement illogical, unconvincing, and unbelievable. Once this happens, you'll realize that anxiety doesn't have to keep going. You have interrupted the pattern and can now think about what you would rather hear yourself say inside your head.

Reframing

This method involves backing up to the beginning thought or belief that started your worry. It turns around unhelpful and possibly untrue beliefs about yourself. You can review the section on cognitive distortions for a refresher on reframing.

It is simple, yet it has profound effects. The reason we suffer is because we believe the thoughts we are thinking are true.

If we are always walking around with different assumptions about the world and beliefs that make us feel bad, shouldn't we make sure they are at least valid thoughts?

Ask these questions and then do a turn-around, which is a way of inverting a belief.

The first step is to determine the thought that is running through your head right before anxiety starts. Simply ask yourself, "How am I thinking about this situation or myself that has me feeling anxious?"

For instance, the person you are dating doesn't text you back for an hour, so you think your relationship is doomed and you are going to break up. You may be thinking and believing, "I'm a failure, no one wants me." Notice how believing this thought makes you feel, and how that feeling makes you act or react.

Notice how you jumped to this conclusion. You automatically predicted a negative outcome when there may be little to no evidence to support it. Next, ask yourself, "Is there any evidence to suggest this is true?" Now invert the thought. "They are probably busy and can't respond to my text right now."

When this happens, the original negative belief loses most of its anxiety-producing power.

It seems too simple and obvious, but when you use it to counter one of your self-defeating beliefs, you'll realize it has a direct affect on how you feel.

You will find that even for little things, when you turn your thoughts around, it makes a tremendous difference.

Use and practice the techniques in the Toolkit daily. By becoming familiar and comfortable with these techniques you will be able to quickly and easily use them to combat anxiety if it arises.

Whenever you feel any anxious feelings start to develop, immediately use the techniques in the Toolkit. You will interrupt the anxiety and re-route your neural pathways to a positive and peaceful place. By repeatedly interrupting anxiety and changing your neural pathways you will not be affected by situations, or thoughts that used to trigger anxiety.

CHAPTER 11

How long does it take to form a new habit and change a neural pathway?

Your anxiety has been with you for a long time. It may even be years in the making. You are likely wondering how long it will take to eliminate it completely. You may even be doing some mental math to determine the exact date that your anxiety will no longer exist.

You have likely come across the assertion that it takes 21 days to develop a new habit, but this often-repeated statistic is questionable – especially when it comes to developing a new habit like mindfulness. Where did this 21-day myth come from?

In the 1950s a plastic surgeon named Maxwell Maltz began noticing a strange pattern among his patients. When Maltz performed an operation — like a nose job, for example — he found that it took the patient about 21 days to get used to seeing their new face. Similarly, when a patient had an arm or a leg amputated, Maltz noticed that the patient would sense a phantom limb for about 21 days before adjusting to the new situation.

These experiences prompted Maltz to think about his own adjustment period to changes and new behaviours, and he noticed that it also took himself about 21 days to form a new habit. Maltz wrote about these experiences and said, "These, and many other commonly observed phenomena tend to show that it requires a minimum of about 21 days for an old mental image to dissolve and a new one to jell."

In 1960, Maltz published that quote and his other thoughts on behaviour change in a book called *Psycho-Cybernetics*. The book went on to become a blockbuster hit, selling more than 30 million copies.

And that's when the problem started.

You see, in the decades that followed, Maltz's work influenced nearly every major "self-help" professional. And as more people recited Maltz's story – like a very long game of "Telephone" – people began to forget that he said "a minimum of about 21 days" and shortened it to: "It takes 21 days to form a new habit."

And that's how society started spreading the common myth that it takes 21 days to form a new habit (or 30 days or some other magic number). It is remarkable how often these timelines are quoted as statistical facts. This is a dangerous lesson: If enough people say something enough times, then everyone else starts to believe it.

It makes sense why the "21 days" myth would spread. It is easy to understand. The time frame is short enough to be inspiring, but long enough to be believable. And who wouldn't like the idea of changing one's life in just three weeks?

But the problem is that Maxwell Maltz was simply observing what was going on around him; he wasn't making a statement of fact. Furthermore, he made sure to say that this was the minimum amount of time needed to adapt to a new change.

So, what's the real answer? How long does it take to form a habit? How long does it take to break a bad habit? Is there any science to back this up? And what does all of this mean for you and me?

Phillippa Lally is a health psychology researcher at University College London. In a study published in the *European Journal of Social Psychology*, Lally and her research team decided to figure out just how long it actually takes to form a habit.

The study examined the habits of 96 people over a 12-week period. Each person chose one new habit to adopt for the 12 weeks and reported each day on whether or not they did the behaviour and how automatic the behaviour felt.

Some people chose simple habits like drinking a bottle of water with lunch. Others chose more difficult tasks like running for 15 minutes before dinner. At the end of the 12 weeks, the researchers analyzed the data to determine how long it took each person to go from starting a new behaviour to automatically doing it.

The answer?

On average, it takes more than 2 months before a new behaviour becomes automatic — 66 days to be exact. Furthermore, how long it takes a new habit to form can vary widely depending on the behaviour, the person, and the circumstances. In Lally's study, it took anywhere from 18 days to 254 days for people to form a new habit.

In other words, if you want to set your expectations appropriately, the truth is that it will probably take you anywhere from two months to eight months to build a new behaviour into your life — not 21 days.

Interestingly, the researchers also found that "missing one opportunity to perform the behaviour did not materially affect the habit formation process." In other words, it doesn't matter if you mess up every now and then. Building better habits is not an all-or-nothing process.

Finding inspiration

Before you let this dishearten you, let's talk about three reasons why this research is actually inspiring.

First, there is no reason to get down on yourself if you try something for a few weeks and it doesn't become a habit. It is supposed to take longer than that! There is no need to judge yourself if you can't master a behaviour in 21 short days. Learn to love your audio recording. Enjoy the mindfulness practice, the relaxation, and the reframing. Embrace the long, slow walk to calmness and focus.

Second, you don't have to be perfect. Making a mistake once or twice has no measurable impact on your long-term habits. This is why you should not treat yourself like a failure, give yourself permission to make mistakes, and develop strategies for getting back on track quickly.

Third, embracing longer timelines can help us realize that habits are a process and not an event. All of the "21 days" hype can make it really easy to think, "Oh, I'll just do this, and it'll be done." But habits never work that way. You have to embrace the process. You have to commit to the system.

Understanding this from the beginning makes it easier to manage your expectations and commit to making small, incremental improvements – rather than pressuring yourself into thinking that you have to do it all at once.

Where to go from here

At the end of the day, how long it takes to eliminate your anxiety doesn't really matter that much. Whether it takes 50 days or 500 days, you have to put in the work either way. The only way to get to Day 500 is to start with Day 1. So, forget about the number and focus on getting started.

The anxiety state can be broken and the brain rewired to deal with the emotions of being human. By reframing anxious thoughts and creating new more positive ones, you can break the cycle of anxiety and create new neural pathways.

Now you have an understanding of anxiety, how your mind works, and the amazing power of neural plasticity. Remember that the brain does not distinguish whether or not something is real to create a neural pathway. That is why the negative self-talk in your head has been so effective in creating anxiety.

In order to be successful in eliminating your anxiety, your new neural pathways must be strong. To make the pathway strong listen to the audio recording daily and interrupt anxiety patterns with the exercises in your Toolkit every time you feel anxiety coming on. Before you know it, your anxiety will be eliminated.

Maintenance

Congratulations on making permanent, positive changes in your life. You have been on a tremendous journey. Celebrate your commitment to yourself and to taking your life back.

After your anxiety subsides, you will find that you will not need to use the Toolkit or listen to the audio recording every night.

The audio recording and techniques in the Toolkit will always be there to help you, and you can use them at any time should you feel the need arise or if you would like to have a little refresher to strengthen your new anxiety free neural pathways.

SOURCES

"Anxiety Disorders."https://www.mayoclinic.org/diseases-conditions/
    anxiety/symptoms-causes/syc-20350961   (accessed February
    1, 2020).

"Anxiety Statistics, Facts, Information." https://www.anxietycentre.com/
    anxiety-statistics-information.shtml (accessed February 1, 2020).

Carson, Shawn and Tiers, Melissa. *Keeping the Brain in Mind*, New York,
    Changing Mind Publishing, 2014

Chapman, Robin. *The Clinical Use of Hypnosis in Cognitive Behaviour
    Therapy* New York, NY: Springer Publishing Company, 2006.

Cherry, Kendra. "How Consolidation Turns Short-Term Memories
    into Long Term Ones". https://www.verywellmind.com/what-is-
    memory-consolidation-2795355 (accessed Jan.17, 2020).

Clear, James. "The Evolution of Anxiety: Why We Worry and What to do
    About It." https://jamesclear.com/evolution-of-anxiety (accessed
    July 22, 2020).

Clear, James. "How Long does it Actually Take to Form a New Habit?
    (Backed by Science)" https://jamesclear.com/new-habit (accessed
    July 22, 2020).

Cocchimiglio, Sarah. "Cognitive Distortions: Is your Mind Playing
    Tricks on You?" https://www.betterhelp.com/advice/general/

cognitive-distortions-is-your-mind-playing-tricks-on-you/ (accessed March 13, 2020).

"Cognitive Behaviour Therapy." http://anxietycanada.com/articles/ cognitive-behaviour-therapy-cbt/(accessed March 13, 2020).

Coppard, Vanessa. "Globally, 1 in 13 Suffers from Anxiety." https://www. futurity.org/globally-1-in-13-suffers-from-anxiety/ (accessed September 20, 2020).

Daitch, Carolyn. *Affect Regulation Toolbox*. New York, NY:W.W.Norton & Company, 2007

Daitch, Carolyn. "Cognitive Behavioural Therapy, Mindfulness and Hypnosis as Treatment Methods for Generalized Anxiety Disorder", 2018

"Distortions of Memory" https://www.sparknotes.com/psychology/ psych101/memory/section6/page/2/ (accessed May 14, 2020).

"Epidemiology of Anxiety Disorders in the 21st Century" https://www. ncbi.nlm.nih.gov/pmc/articles/PMC4610617/ (accessed March 7, 2020)

"Even a Single Mindfulness Meditation Session can Reduce Anxiety" https://www.sciencedaily.com/releases/2018/04/180423135048. htm (accessed June 12, 2020).

"Facts & Statistics, Anxiety and Depression Association of America." https://adaa.org/about-adaa/press-room/facts-statistics, (accessed February 8, 2020).

Felman, Adam. "What Causes Anxiety." https://www.medicalnewstoday. com/articles/323456.php (accessed February 8, 2020).

Felton, Kathleen. "These Groups are Most at Risk for Anxiety Disorders." https://www.health.com/anxiety/anxiety-disorders-women (accessed February 9, 2020).

Firestone, Dr. Lisa. "Is Your Past Controlling Your Life?" Psychologytoday. com/us/blog/compassion-matters/201611/is-your-past-control-ling-your-life (accessed May 7, 2020).

Fredete, Catherine & El-Baalbaki, Ghassan & Neron, Sylvain & Palardy, Veronique. *Using Hypnosis in the Treatment of Anxiety Disorders: Pros and Cons* chapter 3, 6, 7 1996) 399 (March 20, 2013)

Frye, Devon. "Why anxiety goes untreated." *Psychology Today*, (August 2020)

Gander, Kashmira. "Millennials Are the Most Anxious Generation, New Research Shows" https://www.newsweek.com/millennials-most-anxious-generation-new-research-shows-917095 (accessed July 16, 2020).

Geddes, Linda. "Why We Worry: Understanding Anxiety and How to Help It." https://www.newscientist.com/article/mg23230940-300-why-we-worry-understanding-anxiety-and-how-to-help-it/ (accessed February 9, 2020).

"Generalized Anxiety Disorder." https://www.mayoclinic.org/diseases-conditions/generalized-anxiety-disorder/diagnosis-treatment/drc-20361045 (accessed February 8, 2020).

Loftus EF & Palmer JC. 1974 "Reconstruction of automobile destruction; an example of the interaction between language and memory". *Journal of Verbal Learning and Verbal Behaviour*; 13(50): 585–9

Loppie, Samantha & Reading, Charlotte & de Leeuw, Sarah, "Aboriginal Experiences with Racism and Its Impacts" https://www.ccnsa-nccah.ca/docs/determinants/FS-AboriginalExperiencesRacismImpacts-Loppie-Reading-deLeeuw-EN.pdf

Lynn, Steven & Kirsch, Irving & Rhue, Judith. *Casebook of Clinical Hypnosis*. American Psychological Association, 1996.

Mayberg HS, et al. 2002 "The functional neuroanatomy of the placebo effect". *American Journal of Psychiatry*; 159(5): 728–37

McCloskey M, et al. 1988 "Is there a special flashbulb-memory mechanism?" *Journal of Experimental Psychology: General*; 117(2): 171–181

"Memory Distortions" https://courses.lumenlearning.com/boundless-psychology/chapter/memory-disto (accessed May 4, 2020).

"Mood and Anxiety Disorders in Canada." https://www.canada.ca/en/public-health/services/publications/diseases-conditions/mood-anxiety-disorders-canada.html (accessed February 9, 2020).

Morrison, *DSM-5 Made Easy: The Clinicians Guide to Diagnosis*. New York: The Guilford Press, 2014.

Nongard, Dr. Richard & Woods, Kelly 2018: *Reframing Hypnotherapy, Evidence-Based Techniques for Your Next Hypnosis Session.* Scottsdale, AZ: Peachtree Professional Education.

Remes, Olivia. "Women are Far More Anxious than Men – Here's the Science." https://theconversation.com/women-are-far-more-anxious-than-men-heres-the-science (accessed March 11, 2020).

Riopel, Leslie. "Mindfulness and the Brain: What does Research and Neuroscience Say?" https://positivepsychology.com/mindfulness-brain-research-neuroscience/ (accessed March 11, 2020).

Rodman, Dr. Samantha. "Raised by Anxious Parents? Here's how it Might be Affecting Your Mental Health." https://www.talkspace.com/blog/raised-by-anxious-parents-heres-how-it-might-be-affecting-your-mental-health/(accessed April 4, 2020).

"Schema" http://changingminds.org/explanations/theories/schema.htm (accessed June 16, 2020).

Schwartz JM, et al.1996 "Systematic changes in cerebral glucose metabolic rate after successful behaviour modification treatment of obsessive-compulsive disorder." *Archives of General Psychiatry*; 53(2): 109-13 (accessed July 22, 2020).

Sinicki, Adam. "How Your Memory Changes Every Time You Access It" https://www.healthguidance.org/entry/17590/1/how-your-memory-changes-every-time-you-access-it.html (accessed March 18, 2020).

Slater, Erika. "Here's What Hypnosis does to the Brain – What Happens to your Brain on Hypnosis Revealed" https://www.freeatlasthypnosis.com/heres-hypnosis-does-brain-happens-your-brain-on-hypnosis-revealed/ (accessed April 8, 2020).

"10 Commons Symptoms of Anxiety Disorder". https://facty.com/conditions/anxiety-disorder/10-common-symptoms-of-anxiety-disorder/10/(accessed February 9, 2020).

Thorpe, JR. "This is Why Women are More Prone to Anxiety than Men, According to a New Study". https://www.bustle.com/p/why-women-are-more-prone-to-anxiety-than-men-according-to-a-new-study (accessed March 18, 2020).

Tiers, Melissa. *The Anti-Anxiety Toolkit*, New York, NY: Tiers 2011.

"Wellbeing Part Two: 5 Quick Mindfulness Exercises for the Workplace" https://www.regus.co.uk/work-uk/wellbeing-part-two-5-quick-mindfulness-exercises-workplace/ (accessed April 19, 2020).

"Why 75 Percent of Anxiety Sufferers Fail to get Proper Care." https://www.psychologytoday.com/ca/blog/psychiatry-the-people/201808/why-75-percent-anxiety-sufferers-fail-get-proper-care (accessed May 14, 2020).

Wignall, Nick. "Understanding Anxiety: The Complete Beginners's Guide." http://workplacementalhealth.org/News-Events/News-Listing/Anxiety-Disorders-Why-They-Matter (accessed February 6, 2020).

Printed in Canada